BOTANICAL
SHAKESPEARE

BOTANICAL
SHAKESPEARE

———◆·✕·◆———

AN ILLUSTRATED
COMPENDIUM
of All the Flowers, Fruits, Herbs,
Trees, Seeds, and Grasses Cited by the
World's Greatest Playwright

Written and Edited
by
GERIT QUEALY

Conceived and Illustrated
by
SUMIÉ HASEGAWA-COLLINS

With a Foreword
by
HELEN MIRREN

To Allison Kyle Leopold for her unflagging mentorship and friendship
[and launch into garden writing] and Eloïse Watt for creating the Shakespeare Workout,
a gym for the universe of verse, and playground for Shakespeare geeks galore

—Gerit Quealy

To Simon, Brad, Sharon, Adam, and Fred for all their help and support

—Sumié Hasegawa-Collins

Botanical Shakespeare
Text © 2017 by Gerit Quealy and Sumié Hasegawa-Collins
Illustrations © 2017 by Gerit Quealy and Sumié Hasegawa-Collins
Foreword © 2017 by Helen Mirren

HarperCollins books may be purchased for educational, business, or sales promotional use.
For information please email the Special Markets Department at SPsales@harpercollins.com.

HarperCollins Publishers
www.harpercollins.com

Distributed throughout the world by
HarperCollins Publishers
195 Broadway
New York, NY 10007

ISBN 978-0-06-246989-2
Library of Congress Control Number 2016951429

Printed in Italy

First Printing, 2017

24 RTLO 7

Bouquet paintings created by the artist to illustrate some of the more famous
plant-laden passages grace the introductory pages of this book:

page 2: B U R G U N D Y, Henry V [Act V, sc. 2]

page 5: S ONG OF S P R I N G , Love's Labour's Lost [Act V, sc. 2]

page 8: O B E R O N , A Midsummer Night's Dream [Act II, sc. 1]

page 10: O P H E L I A , Hamlet [Act IV, sc. 5]

Yet Nature is made better by no mean
But Nature makes that mean: so, over that Art
Which you say adds to Nature, is an Art
That Nature makes.
You see, sweet maid, we marry
A gentler scion to the wildest stock,
And make conceive a bark of baser kind
By bud of nobler race: this is an Art
Which does mend Nature, change it rather, but
The ART itself is NATURE.

—*Winter's Tale* [Act IV, Scene 4]

CONTENTS

FOREWORD

———•◦•◦•———

This graceful volume is the marriage of Shakespeare's words about plants and the plants themselves. It beautifully combines my love of Shakespeare and of gardening. Seeing what each plant looks like, their faces if you will, is fascinating, and incredibly helpful, especially with the more obscure ones.

My penchant for gardening came during my time with the Royal Shakespeare Company in Stratford—the physicality of the material and the material world of plants sort of converged. There I developed a passion for the countryside—the gold and green of the landscape, the changing colours and textures of the seasons, the scent of damp earth and pungent wildflowers.

It's the experience of each that provides the thrill: getting your hands dirty, diving down to the root of it all, finding the real joy of growth. "Joy's soul lies in the doing," says Shakespeare's Cressida, and it's true.

Nature has become a passion and a tonic for me so finding a way to keep it close is a priority [I even made a garden outside my trailer in Lithuania while shooting *Elizabeth I*]. It satisfies what I call my appetite for solitude.

How delightful then that this elegant book contains all of Shakespeare's words about plants beside exquisite drawings of the plants themselves. You can sit with it in solitude and have a direct experience of each plant. You can almost touch or smell each one. Maybe it will make you want to do that—feel the spiky thorns of the rose or the fuzzy heads of burdock. I hope so. I love the fact that the olives I grow in my garden appear in six different plays, plus a sonnet [107]: "Peace proclaims Olives of endless age."

—Helen Mirren

INTRODUCTION

He will work you any Flower to the life, as like it
as if it grew in the very place;
and being a delicate perfumer
he will give it you his perfect and natural Savour.

—from *Sir Gyles Goosecappe,* by George Chapman

Lawyers claim Shakespeare was a lawyer, doctors think he was medically trained, actors assume he was a thespian, soldiers, sailors, and astronomers all claim a kindred spirit. So it should be no surprise that knowledgeable gardeners think the Bard's extensive use of botanical references would qualify him as a Master Gardener.

Playwright Ben Jonson, Shakespeare's eulogist of sorts, said he was "not of an Age, but for all Time." He might have added, "for all professions." Ben's 1623 prognostication proved true enough—the immortal Bard's work and wit are probably more popular and pored over than those of any other writer throughout history.

Just as Shakespeare's words have fallen on fertile ground, so are they fertile ground themselves for a bounty of botany. Professional horticulturalists, gardening hobbyists, and nature lovers in general all share a fascination for the vast array of flowers, fruits, grains, grasses, seeds and weeds, plants and trees, herbs, spices, and vegetables sprouting in Shakespeare's plays and sonnets—roughly 175 specific mentions, with even more general references and commentary on planting, pruning, growing, grafting, weeding, seeding, folklore galore, and tributes, naturally:

. . . tongues in trees, books in the running brooks,
Sermons in stones and good in every thing.

Even the sinister side of plants—dangerous poisons, painful nettles and thorns, or the threatening approach of Birnam Wood—holds thrall.

I will not be afraid of death and bane,
Till Birnam forest come to Dunsinane.

Casual mentions of plants are interlaced everywhere; the *bane* tucked in the above quotation is a succinct rhyme but also no doubt a truncated version of either Wolfsbane or Henbane, deadly poisons perfectly at home in the dark world that is *Macbeth*.

THERE WAS SOMETHING ABOUT ELIZABETH . . .

Perhaps this fertile ground owes more to the reign of Elizabeth than to anything else. Her ascension to the throne in 1558 marked a sort of steadying of the severe pendulum swings put in motion by her father, Henry VIII, when he broke with the church in Rome. That shock was still reverberating through the populace when first the Evangelion Edward VI, then his Catholic sister, who became known as Bloody Mary, succeeded in stretching the country to the extremes of religious fervor. The highly educated, peaceable, and pleasure-loving Elizabeth stayed that pendulum insomuch as she could. She seeded England with a passion for learning; poetry fused with the classics flourished, and the new entertainment of plays. Publishing went into overdrive, first with translations of popular material from Europe, which included botany books, then with homegrown versions in just about every genre. Which is why this era is known as the Early Modern period, because it is essentially the community from which our current society springs. In short, she created a culture in which investigation, discovery, experimentation, and creativity blossomed. A sort of garden plan to foster a Renaissance at any time.

THE BIRTH OF BOTANICALS

Shakespeare's relationship to plants illustrates an expansive awareness of botany coupled with a colloquial familiarity. That, grafted with his unmatched skill for creating metaphorical connections and interweaving substantive philosophy, made for some of the most memorable lines in literature. It is interesting to note that the nascent variety of botanical and herbal books of the period were in Latin or Greek—so showing off your garden was a way to flaunt your smarts. As Queen Elizabeth's reign progressed, lust for more knowledge and know-how about plants steadily rose, and vernacular garden books entered the market in ever-increasing numbers: William Turner, considered the father of scientific botany in England, had a hit with his *A New Herball*. Thomas Hill's *Profitable Arte of Gardening* in 1563, Hugh Platt's *Floraes Paradis* [in English but poshed up with a Latin title], *A niewe Herball* from botanist Henry Lyte in 1578, Thomas Tusser's 1557 *A Hundreth Good Pointes of Husbandrie* swelled to an alarming *Five Hundred Pointes . . .* by 1573—all best-sellers. A quarto copy of *A Treatise of The Arte of Graffing and Planting Trees* was so popular it went into five reprints. "Green desire," with its promise of status, beauty, order, and magic, was rampant.

The *Newe Jewell of Health*, a translation of Swiss botanist Conrad Gesner's work, was proffered by the sixteenth-century physician George Baker. He, in turn, wrote the foreword for a 1597 book that is considered a primary source for Shakespeare's extensive botanical knowledge: John Gerard's *Herball, or Generall Historie of Plantes*.

The *Herball* remained unsurpassed for decades; even when apothecary John Parkinson's comprehensive *Theatrum Botanicum* came along, in 1640, it was not entirely supplanted. The innate charm, pervasive information, personal experience, and hat-tips to poetry woven throughout Gerard's *Herball* made it a pleasant companion as well as an authoritative source; it is a primary resource for this book. Baker, in his prefatory dedication, expresses amazement at the compendious nature of the tome:

> *The Author of this book, his great pains,*
> *his no less expenses in travelling far and near for the attaining of his*
> *skill have been extraordinary . . . not only to have them brought, but*
> *hath procured by his excellent knowledge to have them growing in his garden, . . .*
> *for there shall you see all manner of strange trees, herbs, roots, plants, flowers*
> *and other such rare things, that it would make a man wonder how one of his degree,*
> *not having the purse of a number, could ever accomplish the same.*
> *I protest upon my conscience, I do not think for the*
> *knowledge of Plants, that he is inferior to any . . .*

An ideal resource for Shakespeare. And in fact, there may be direct proof that this is true. One researcher found some curious anomalies in the "Song of Spring," a.k.a. "Cuckoo's Song," in *Love's Labour's Lost*:

> *. . . And Ladie-smockes all silver white,*
> *And Cuckow-buds of yellow hew . . .*

Scholars over the years have assumed that many of the plant, and especially flower, names in Shakespeare must be local Warwickshire vernacular [which proved untrue] or his own coinages, but this researcher noted the song was wrong: "Ladie-smockes are pale lilac not silver-white" and "Cuckow-buds are not yellow!" Turning to Gerard's *Herball* for insight, he found in chapter 18, Book II: "Of wilde water cresses or Cuckow flowers" there are six varieties, "all but one are termed ladie smockes. The 5th variety is described as follows: 5. Milke white Ladie smockes hath stalkes rising immediately from the roote, . . . The flowers growe at the top, made of fower leaves of a yellowish colour." Gerard describes habitat and flowering time: "These kinds of Cuckowe flowers, grow not so much in waters as they do in moist medowes . . . flower for the most part in Aprill and Maie, when the Cucowe doth begin to sing her pleasant notes without stammering." He then lists their foreign names, and "in English Cuckowe flowers . . . [but] at the Namptwich in Cheshire where I had my beginning, Ladie smockes, which hath given me cause to christen it after my countrie fashion." Illustrating that Shakespeare's unique terms *come directly* out of Gerard. In her engaging *A Shakespearean Botanical*, renowned garden author Margaret Willes posits the possibility of acquaintance between playwright and botanist, because Gerard records finding a double-form "butterflower" while walking with a friend to "the Theatre"—such was the stage in Shoreditch called that was run by Richard Burbage, until they tore it down in 1598 to build the Globe with its timbers.

SHAKESPEARE AND MEDICINE

Shakespeare's knowledge of "physick," as it was then called, has amazed and intrigued the medical profession for centuries. Theodore Dalrymple, the pseudonym for a retired prison physician and psychiatrist, has been quoted as saying,

The Bard's uncanny grasp of what ails us puts much of modern medicine to shame.

Research has uncovered the fact that Shakespeare seemed aware of the circulation of the blood in the body before it was "officially" discovered. Helena, the heroine of *All's Well That Ends Well*, is an accomplished herbalist, having learned her father's trade at his knee, as it were [although curiously, she doesn't mention any herbal names, only Briers and Thorns]. She sees the King's disease as an opportunity to apply her knowledge, thereby winning her choice of husband [albeit an unwilling one]. Professor Joseph Wagner of Kent State University has identified the source of the King's pain which Helena's herbal ministrations heal, illustrating once again Shakespeare's cognizance of the intrinsic connection between botanical and medical expertise.

Afflictions of the body such as scurvy, gout, rheumatism, and venereal disease punctuate the canon, along with the medicinal plants to help cure them. Some of the above-mentioned botanical books focused on their medical applications as well, and a coterie of men and women were well versed in their usage, such as Cambridge scholar and diplomat Sir Thomas Smith, as well as the Countess of Arundel and the Countess of Kent—the ministrations of upper-class medicine women were much the same as a wisewoman's healing practice, according to Rebecca Laroche, author of *Medical Authority and Englishwomen's Herbal Texts, 1550—1650*. Her assessment: "The recipe that *Macbeth*'s witches incant is astonishingly accurate."

SHAKESPEARE, PLANTS, AND SEX

Shakespeare's use of plants runs the gamut from the sublime ["a Rose by any other name . . ."] to the satirical: the 'focative caret' in *Merry Wives of Windsor*'s Latin lesson is called a "good root" by Mistress Quickly, punning on the vegetable homonym of course, but also entering sexual territory: "root" also refers to the male member; "caret" literally means 'what's missing'; and the top greens of wild carrots were ancient applications for contraception, stimulants for menses, and abortifacients. In fact, the entire scene is loaded with sex jokes; paired with the caret/carrot, having Parson Evans mispronounce "vocative" with an "f" is just Shakespeare's version of the f-bomb.

The Gooseberry too lends itself to sexual punning, for instance, Biron's "green goose" reference in *Love's Labour's Lost* acknowledges, yes, a gooseberry is green, but the women in brothels near the Bishop's palace in Southwark were known as Winchester geese, so the green goose can also refer to a new/young prostitute.

Shakespeare's frequent use of plants metaphorically delves into all manner of Elizabethan sexual practices [well, not *just* Elizabethan]. The language may seem a little opaque, but seeing what the plants being referenced actually look like is a big help. Nowhere is this more apparent than with the Medlar [see page 112]. Scholars have often conjectured as to whether Mercutio is homosexual, and possibly in love with Romeo. One look at the Medlar—Shakespeare only cites the fruit, never the tree or flower—and it is perhaps easier to understand the speculation. In fact this obscure fruit may be the origin of the word *fruit* used as an epithet for *gay*. Awareness of these allusions, and especially the ability to cross-reference where they appear, will let you in on the conversation—and help you get the jokes.

SHAKESPEARE THE LOCAVORE

Today's organic, locally grown food movement might have stumped Shakespeare; in the sixteenth century this "trend" was the norm. Exotic imports were exciting—Nutmeg and Ginger became staple ingredients; recipes from foreign countries, particularly Italy, were wildly popular, as discussed in *Shakespeare's Kitchen* by Francine Segan. But the staples of the table and larder in Shakespeare's day were an abundance of locally sourced foods, herbs, grains, seeds, and spices. Although people ate far more meat than vegetables at this time, common folk were savvy about growing foods for overwintering: drying Peas and Beans, Plums to Prunes, potherbs with grain for pottage; pickling and preserving were mainstay maneuvers for keeping the pantry stocked during lean months, especially because crop failures could be disastrous [see Corn, page 191, regarding the corn rebellions].

Kitchen gardens, too, proliferated during the Elizabethan horticultural boom, primarily the province of women—men handled the orchards. Peacetime meant growth, literally as well as figuratively: Flowers planted for medicine now bloomed for beauty too, and many were edible. New books on "husbandrie" and "cookery," such as the 1577 *Gardener's Labyrinth*, were best-sellers—the fact that they were written in English, coupled with the exponential increase in literacy, was certainly a significant element of their success.

THE PLANT PORTRAITS

Artist Sumié Hasegawa-Collins trained as a concert pianist during her childhood in Tokyo. Always having to be mindful of her hands, she found that drawing and painting were among the few recreational outlets available. Years later, after winning a prize in graphic design and then moving to America, where she became a textile designer, she found herself designing costumes for her husband's Bond Street Theatre outdoor productions of *A Shakespeare Party*, a compilation of scenes from the plays. Always acutely aware of nature, she began to notice the abundance of plants peppering the lines and songs, and they started to germinate in her artistic consciousness. From frequent trips to the New York Botanical Garden in the Bronx, all the way to Kew Gardens in outer London, she learned to meld her expertise in watercolor technique with the demands of botanical rendering. It has been a passion spanning decades to research and represent every last leaf and stem, peel and petal of Shakespeare's botanical universe.

WEEDING THE WORDS

Less Balm, no Angelica. Iris of sorts.

Beyond the familiar quotes often posted [and misquoted] on Facebook lies the world of actors and scholars forever arguing about issues of interpretation. A rose may be a rose to Gertrude Stein, but in Shakespeare it can be rife with meaning—love, beauty, dynasty, scent, color, and danger [those thorns!]. Looking at his works through a specific lens, such as that of plants, yields a fresh crop of insights—and a fresh field of debate. Much like the roiling underbelly of the serene suburban garden in David Lynch's cult film *Blue Velvet,* the perfect and polished surface of Shakespeare masks a tempest of contention about meaning and authorial intent—are Leather-coats Apples or seeds? Is Insane Root Hamlet's poison? And what about the Peony!

Similarly, a number of characters with plant names can pose a conundrum—Peter Quince in *A Midsummer Night's Dream,* or Costard in *Love's Labour's Lost.* What about the mysterious Angelica in *Romeo and Juliet*? Is it the Nurse's given name, or perhaps an offstage kitchen wench doing Lord Capulet's bidding? Some might convince you the "name" is strategic "product placement" amidst the marriage feast preparations for its edible and medicinal qualities ... so, while we don't include it in the body of the book, the herb can be seen here on page 18, at the close of this Introduction. The same holds true for Henry Pimpernell from the Induction scene of *Taming of the Shrew*—is his name some sort of floral clue, or does it simply add a dash of color to an opaque character? We included the plant on page 6 in case that famous Scarlet Pimpernel from a centuries-later novel happened to launch his career in Shakespeare. Iris, the goddess of the rainbow, appears or is mentioned in a number of plays, although the flower itself is never mentioned—and yet it *is* in evidence as the Flower-de-luce and Flag.

General vs. Specific

Some judicious pruning of the quotes was done to separate plant from metaphor—with a little wiggle room for debate. BALM [sometimes Balsam or Balsamum] became a generic term for succor, or royal anointment [the 'balm of my poor eyes' are tears, not the plant], so over half of those quotes don't make the cut and some that are included might be contestable. It is in fact very difficult to calculate precisely how many plants are mentioned in Shakespeare because even within our specific Plant Portraits are interspersed arguably general terms: CORN can mean all manner of grain; GRASSES umbrellas a number of plants, such as Fescue; even ROSE [and certainly THORNS] starts to seem generic after the multitudinous mentions of this presumed favorite flower, especially when under that heading there are specific Roses cited. So, we did not illustrate every bramble and brake. And we were mindful not to fall for "false flowers"—sometimes a *mint* is a place to forge coins, *rose* is a verb, *elder* a senior citizen, and a *palm* just the inside of a royal wave.

ALL LATIN AND FENUGREEK

There is no fenugreek [a medicinal and culinary herb] in Shakespeare, but there *is* plenty of Greek [as settings and sources for some of the plots]. And there is a lot of Latin. But since Carl Linnaeus wasn't yet on the scene, neither was the systematic Latin nomenclature he developed for botanical identification. Which is not to say there wasn't one, although there wasn't *one*—various systems were devised by different sects of monks, for instance, who didn't talk to each other [if they talked at all], so the naming process was inconsistent, inaccurate, and sometimes just confusing [Gerard's *Herball* is a testament to this]. Jacques le Moyne de Morgues [great name], a French artist who actually travelled to Florida in 1564, took pains to make a color catalog in 1586 [only three exist in the world today] of many common flowers and fruits, noting their names in Latin, as well as French, German, and English; he dedicated it to Mary Sidney Herbert, Countess of Pembroke, another prominent English poet of the time.

Ergo, since Shakespeare didn't really use Latin signifiers, we don't either—except in rare cases such as Rose, to allow a means of differentiation.

HOW TO USE THIS BOOK

Along with Gerard's *Herball,* Canon Henry Ellacombe's exhaustive *The plant-lore and garden-craft of Shakespeare,* compiled in the mid- to late 1800s, was a primary source for this book. The well-named reverend combed through all those words words words to find every single plant mention without the Internet! [He missed some, but remarkably few.] *Shakespeare's Plants and Gardens—A Dictionary* [in the Arden series], by Vivian Thomas and Nicki Faircloth, was a last-minute boon. These materials also cover more general references and gardening terminology, such as pruning, plowing, grafting, odiferous terms, even flap-dragon, a game involving flaming raisins [hey, there wasn't a lot to do].

Our aim was to put a "face" with the plant name, paired with all the attendant quotes, so you could better see the Bard's interior landscape, if you will. I expect there will be debate over a chosen plant here and there, or a missed quote. Much like the couched *bane* in the aforementioned quote from *Macbeth,* it was fun to find *goose* a short form for *gooseberry,* used for its color, essentially to convey "you look a little green" today. Scavenger hunting for poetic plants is a forager's feast.

But for pure pleasure: Pick out a quick quote for your favorite Aunt Rose, or a verdant cluster of lilting lines for a sweetheart, a botanically based insult for an enemy, a remembrance of a favorite herb or flower for a treasured friend; map out plans for a garden plot or pot based on your favorite play or characters, or assemble a bouquet based on subliminal messages: While Nutmeg, Marigold, and Ginger may say "open up to the spice of life," a cluster of Plantain, Parmaceti, and Pomewater promise healing of body and soul.

A note about the poetry: In addition to the Sonnets, included are *Venus and Adonis, Lucrece* [sans *The Rape of* . . . , as per the title page of its first publication in 1594], *The Phoenix and the Turtle, A Lover's Complaint,* and *The Passionate Pilgrim*—although not all of the latter, as scholars have determined that only about five of those poems are "Shakespearean."

The problem with Shakespeare, and yes, there is one, is that he's so familiar that he's too familiar. In the way that you can sometimes ignore or forget about a close friend or family member because they are always there for you. Even little kids seem to know "To be or not to be . . . ," even if they don't know why or how; it's ingrained in the culture. And yet, when you stop, for just a moment [yes, I am going to go there] and smell the flowers, the power of the thought, idea, or emotion can pervade your being, even rock your world. Poet Robert Graves cleverly encapsulates it: "The remarkable thing about Shakespeare is that he's really very good . . . in spite of all the people who say he's very good."

> *Nature herself was proud of his designs,*
> *And joy'd to wear the dressing of his lines!*
>
> —Ben Jonson,
> First Folio of Shakespeare

❧ THE BOTANICALS ❧

Plant Portraits, Alphabetically

AND QUOTES

ACONITUM

HENRY IV

The united vessel of their blood,
Mingled with venom of suggestion—
As, force perforce,
the age will pour it in—
Shall never leak,
though it do work as strong
As ACONITUM
or rash gunpowder.

—*Henry IV, Pt. 2* [Act IV, sc. 4]

ACORN

Mast [*see also Oak**]

PROSPERO

Thy food shall be
The fresh-brook muscles, wither'd roots, and husks
Wherein the ACORN cradled.

—*Tempest* [Act I, sc. 2]

PUCK

All their elves, for fear,
Creep into ACORN-CUPS
and hide them there.

—*A Midsummer Night's Dream* [Act II, sc. 1]

LYSANDER

Get you gone, you dwarf;
You minimus, of hindering knot-grass made;
You bead, you ACORN.

—*A Midsummer Night's Dream* [Act III, sc. 2]

TIMON

The oaks bear MAST, the briers scarlet hips.

—*Timon of Athens* [Act IV, sc. 3]

POSTHUMUS

Like a full-ACORNED boar—
a German one.

—*Cymbeline* [Act II, sc. 5]

CELIA

I found him under a tree
like a dropped ACORN.

—*As You Like It* [Act III, sc. 2]

ADONIS FLOWER

Fritillary

And in his blood
that on the ground lay spill'd,
A PURPLE FLOWER sprung up
CHEQUER'D WITH WHITE,
Resembling well his pale cheeks,
and the blood
Which in round drops
upon their whiteness stood.

—*Venus and Adonis*

ALMOND

THERSITES

The parrot will not do more
for an ALMOND...

—*Troilus and Cressida*
[Act V, sc. 2]

ALOE

And sweetens, in the suffering pangs it bears,
The ALOES of all forces, shocks, and fears.

—*A Lover's Complaint*

APPLE

*Apple-john*Codling*Bitter-sweeting*Pippin*Pomewater*Costard*

SEBASTIAN

I think he will carry this island
home in his pocket
and give it his son for an APPLE.

—*Tempest* [Act II, sc. 1]

ANTONIO

An evil soul producing holy witness
Is like a villain with a smiling cheek,
A goodly APPLE rotten at the heart.

—*Merchant of Venice* [Act I, sc. 3]

ANTONIO

An APPLE cleft in two is not more twin
Than these two creatures.

—*Twelfth Night* [Act V, sc. 1]

HORTENSIO

As you say, there's small choice
in rotten APPLES.

—*Taming of the Shrew* [Act I, sc. 1]

TRANIO

He in countenance
somewhat doth resemble you.

BIONDELLO

As much as an APPLE doth an oyster,
and all one.

—*Taming of the Shrew* [Act IV, sc. 2]

MALVOLIO

Not yet old enough for a man,
nor young enough for a boy;
as a squash is before 'tis a peascod,
for a CODLING when 'tis almost an APPLE.

—*Twelfth Night* [Act I, sc. 5]

ORLEANS

Foolish curs, that run winking
into the mouth of a Russian bear,
and have their heads crushed
like rotten APPLES.

—*Henry V* [Act III, sc. 7]

PORTER

These are the youths
that thunder at a playhouse,
and fight for bitten APPLES . . .

—*Henry VIII* [Act V, sc. 4]

FALSTAFF

My skin hangs about me like
an old lady's loose gown; I am withered
like an old APPLE-JOHN.

—*Henry IV, Pt.* 1 [Act III, sc. 3]

FIRST DRAWER

What the devil hast thou brought here?
APPLE-JOHNS?
Thou knowest Sir John
cannot endure an APPLE-JOHN.

SECOND DRAWER

Thou sayest true; the prince once set a dish of
APPLE-JOHNS before him,
and told him there were five more Sir Johns;
and putting off his hat, said, I will now
take my leave of these six dry,
round, old, withered knights.

—*Henry IV, Pt.* 2 [Act II, sc. 4]

SHALLOW

Nay, you shall see my orchard, where,
in an arbour, we will eat
a last year's PIPPIN of my own graffing,
with a dish of caraways . . .

—*Henry IV, Pt.* 2 [Act V, sc. 3]

MERCUTIO

Thy wit is a very BITTER-SWEETING;
it is a most sharp sauce.

ROMEO

And is it not well served in to a sweet goose?

—*Romeo and Juliet* [Act II, sc. 4]

SIR HUGH EVANS

I will make an end of my dinner.
There's PIPPINS and cheese to come.

—*Merry Wives of Windsor* [Act I, sc. 2]

HOLOFERNES / PEDANT

The deer was, as you know, *sanguis,* in blood;
ripe as a POMEWATER,
who now hangeth like a jewel
in the ear of *cœlo*—the sky, the welkin,
the heaven; and anon falleth
like a CRAB on the face of *terra*—
the soil, the land, the earth.

—*Love's Labour's Lost* [Act IV, sc. 2]

PETRUCHIO

What's this? A sleeve? 'Tis like a demi-cannon.
What, up and down, carved like an
APPLE-TART?

—Taming of the Shrew [Act IV, sc. 3]

How like Eve's APPLE doth thy beauty grow,
If thy sweet virtue answer not thy show!

—Sonnet XCIII

FOOL

Shal't see thy other daughter
will use thee kindly;
for though she's as like this as a CRAB's
like an APPLE, yet I can tell what I can tell.

—King Lear [Act I, sc. 5]

MOTH

A wonder, master! Here's a COSTARD
broken in a shin. . . .

MOTH

By saying that a COSTARD
was broken in a shin. . . .

DON ARMADO

How was there a COSTARD broken in a shin?

—Love's Labour's Lost [Act III, sc. 1]

SIR HUGH EVANS

I will knog his urinals about his knave's
COSTARD when I have
good opportunities for the ork.
'Pless my soul!

—Merry Wives of Windsor [Act III, sc. 1]

FIRST MURDERER

Take him over the COSTARD
with the hilts of thy sword,
and then we will chop him
in the malmsey-butt.

—Richard III [Act I, sc. 4]

EDGAR

Nay, come not near th' old man; keep out,
che vor ye, or ise try whether
your COSTARD or my ballow be the harder.

—King Lear [Act IV, sc. 6]

APRICOT

*Apricocke*Apricocks*

TITANIA

Be kind and courteous to this gentleman;
Hop in his walks, and gambol in his eyes;
Feed him with APRICOCKS and dewberries,
with purple grapes, green figs, and mulberries.

—*A Midsummer Night's Dream* [Act III, sc. 1]

GARDENER

Go, bind thou up yon dangling APRICOCKS,
Which, like unruly children, make their sire
Stoop with oppression of their prodigal weight.

—*Richard II* [Act III, sc. 4]

PALAMON

Would I were,
For all the fortunes of my life hereafter,
Yon little tree, yon blooming APRICOCKE;
How I would spread and fling my wanton arms
In at her window! I would bring her fruit
Fit for the gods to feed on.

—*Two Noble Kinsmen* [Act II, sc. 2]

ARABIAN TREE

OTHELLO

Of one whose subdued eyes,
Albeit unused to the melting mood,
Drop tears as fast as the ARABIAN TREES
Their medicinable gum.

—*Othello* [Act V, sc. 2]

Let the bird of loudest lay,
On the sole ARABIAN TREE,
Herald sad and trumpet be,
To whose sound chaste wings obey.

—*Phoenix and the Turtle*

SEBASTIAN

That in ARABIA
There is ONE TREE, the Phœnix' throne;
one Phœnix
At this hour reigning there.

—*Tempest* [Act III, sc. 3]

ASH

AUFIDIUS

Let me twine
Mine arms about that body, where against
My grained ASH an hundred times hath broke,
And scarr'd the moon with splinters.

—*Coriolanus* [Act IV, sc. 5]

ASPEN

MARCUS

O, had the monster seen those lily hands
Tremble, like ASPEN leaves, upon a lute . . .

—*Titus Andronicus* [Act II, sc. 4]

HOSTESS / MISTRESS QUICKLY

Feel, masters, how I shake. . . .
Yea, in very truth do I,
[as] if I were an ASPEN leaf.

—*Henry IV, Pt. 2* [Act II, sc. 4]

BACHELOR'S BUTTONS / BUDS

HOST OF THE GARTER

What say you to young Master Fenton?
he capers, he dances, he has eyes of youth,
he writes verses, he speaks holiday, he smells
April and May; he will carry't, he will carry't;
'tis in his BUTTONS; he will carry't.

—*Merry Wives of Windsor* [Act III, sc. 2]

TITANIA

An odorous chaplet of sweet summer BUDS
As is in mockery set.

—*A Midsummer Night's Dream* [Act II, sc. 1]

LAERTES

The canker galls the infants of the spring,
Too oft before their BUTTONS be disclosed,
And in the morn and liquid dew of youth
Contagious blastments are most imminent.

—*Hamlet* [Act I, sc. 3]

ARCITE

O Queen Emilia, Fresher than May,
sweeter Than her gold BUTTONS
on the boughs, or all
Th' enameled knacks o' th' mead or garden . . .

—*Two Noble Kinsmen* [Act III, sc. 1]

BALM

*Balsam*Balsamum*

DROMIO OF SYRACUSE

I have conveyed aboard, and I have bought
The oil, the BALSAMUM, and aqua vitæ.

—*Comedy of Errors* [Act IV, sc. 1]

ALCIBIADES

Is this the BALSAM that the usuring Senate
Pours into captains' wounds?

—*Timon of Athens* [Act III, sc. 5]

MISTRESS QUICKLY

The several chairs of order look you scour
With juice of BALM and every precious flower.
Each fair instalment, coat, and several crest,
With loyal blazon, evermore be blest!

—*Merry Wives of Windsor* [Act V, sc. 5]

CLEOPATRA

As sweet as BALM, as soft as air, as gentle.

—*Antony and Cleopatra* [Act V, sc. 2]

And trembling in her passion, calls it BALM,
Earth's sovereign salve to do a goddess good.

—*Venus and Adonis*

And drop sweet BALM in Priam's
painted wound.

—*Lucrece*

BARLEY

IRIS

Ceres, most bounteous lady, thy rich leas
Of wheat, rye, BARLEY, vetches,
oats, and pease.

—Tempest [Act IV, sc. 1]

JAILER'S DAUGHTER

Sometime we go to BARLEY-BREAK,
we of the blessed.

—Two Noble Kinsmen [Act IV, sc. 3]

CONSTABLE

Can sodden water,
A drench for sur-rein'd jades,
their BARLEY broth,
Decoct their cold blood to such valiant heat?

—Henry V [Act III, sc. 5]

BAY / LAUREL

CAPTAIN

'Tis thought the King is dead; we will not stay.
The BAY-TREES in our country
are all wither'd.

—*Richard II* [Act II, sc. 4]

BAWD

Marry come up, my dish of chastity
with rosemary and BAYS!

—*Pericles* [Act IV, sc. 6]

PROLOGUE

O, fan
From me the witless chaff of such a writer
That blasts my BAYS
and my famed works makes lighter.

—*Two Noble Kinsmen* [Prologue 1]

THE VISION

Enter, solemnly tripping one after another,
six personages,
clad in white robes,
wearing on their heads garlands of BAYS,
and golden vizards on their faces,
branches of BAYS or palms in their hands.

—*Henry VIII* [Act IV, sc. 2]

CLARENCE

To whom the heav'ns in thy nativity
adjudged an olive branch
and a LAUREL crown
As likely to be blest in peace and war.

—*Henry VI, Pt. 3* [Act IV, sc. 6]

TITUS

Cometh Andronicus bound
with LAUREL boughs.

—*Titus Andronicus* [Act I, sc. 1]

CLEOPATRA

Upon your sword
sit LAUREL victory and smooth success
bestrewed before your feet.

—*Antony and Cleopatra* [Act I, sc. 3]

ULYSSES

Prerogative of age, crowns, sceptres,
LAURELS.

—*Troilus and Cressida* [Act I, sc. 3]

BEANS

PUCK

When I a fat and BEAN-FED horse beguile.

—*A Midsummer Night's Dream* [Act II, sc. 1]

SECOND CARRIER

Peas and BEANS are as dank here as a dog;
and that is the next way
to give poor jades the bots.

—*Henry IV, Pt.* 1 [Act II, sc. 1]

BILBERRY

PISTOL

Where fires thou find'st unraked
and hearths unswept,
There pinch the maids as blue as BILBERRY—
Our radiant Queen hates sluts and sluttery.

—*Merry Wives of Windsor* [Act V, sc. 5]

BIRCH

DUKE

Fond fathers,
Having bound up
the threatening twigs of BIRCH,
Only to stick it in their children's sight
For terror, not to use, in time the rod
Becomes more mock'd than fear'd . . .

—*Measure for Measure* [Act I, sc. 3]

SCHOOLMASTER

By title pedagogus, that let fall
The BIRCH upon the breeches
of the small ones,
And humble with a ferula the tall ones,
Do here present this machine, or this frame.

—*Two Noble Kinsmen* [Act III, sc. 5]

BLACKBERRIES

Brambles

❦

FALSTAFF

Give you a reason on compulsion?!
If reasons were as plentiful
as BLACKBERRIES, I would give no man
a reason upon compulsion, I.

—*Henry IV, Pt. 1* [Act II, sc. 4]

FALSTAFF

Shall the blessed sun of heaven prove a micher
and eat BLACKBERRIES?

—*Henry IV, Pt. 1* [Act II, sc. 4]

THERSITES

That same dog-fox Ulysses
is not proved worth a BLACKBERRY.

—*Troilus and Cressida* [Act V, sc. 4]

CELIA

There is a man haunts the forest, that abuses
our young plants with carving "Rosalind"
on their barks; hangs odes upon hawthorns
and elegies on BRAMBLES...

—*As You Like It* [Act III, sc. 2]

The THORNY BRAMBLES
and embracing bushes,
As fearful of him, part,
through whom he rushes.

—*Venus and Adonis*

BOX

MARIA

Get ye all three into the BOX-TREE.

—Twelfth Night [Act II, sc. 5]

BRIERS

ARIEL

So I charm'd their ears,
That calf-like they my lowing follow'd through
Tooth'd BRIERS, sharp furzes,
pricking goss, and thorns.

—Tempest [Act IV, sc. 1]

FAIRY

Over hill, over dale, through bush,
through BRIER.

—A Midsummer Night's Dream [Act II, sc. 1]

FLUTE / THISBE

Of colour like the red rose on triumphant BRIER.

—A Midsummer Night's Dream [Act III, sc. 1]

PUCK

I'll lead you about a round,
Through bog, through bush, through BRAKE,
through BRIER.

—*A Midsummer Night's Dream* [Act III, sc. 1]

PUCK

For BRIERS and thorns at their apparel snatch.

—*A Midsummer Night's Dream* [Act III, sc. 2]

HERMIA

Never so weary, never so in woe,
Bedabbled with the dew and torn with BRIERS.

—*A Midsummer Night's Dream* [Act III, sc. 2]

OBERON

Every elf and fairy sprite
Hop as light as bird from BRIER.

—*A Midsummer Night's Dream* [Act V, sc. 1]

ADRIANA

If aught possess thee from me, it is dross,
Usurping ivy, BRIER, or idle moss.

—*Comedy of Errors* [Act II, sc. 2]

PLANTAGENET

From off this BRIER pluck a white rose with me.

—*Henry VI, Pt. 1* [Act II, sc. 4]

ROSALIND

O how full of BRIERS is
this working-day world!

—*As You Like It* [Act I, sc. 3]

HELENA

The time will bring on summer,
When BRIERS shall have leaves
as well as thorns,
And be as sweet as sharp.

—*All's Well That Ends Well* [Act IV, sc. 4]

POLIXENES

I'll have thy beauty scratched with BRIERS.

—*Winter's Tale* [Act IV, sc. 4]

TIMON

The oaks bear mast, the BRIERS scarlet HIPS.

—*Timon of Athens* [Act IV, sc. 3]

CORIOLANUS

Scratches with BRIERS,
scars to move laughter only.

—*Coriolanus* [Act III, sc. 3]

QUINTUS

What subtle hole is this,
Whose mouth is cover'd
with rude-growing BRIERS?

—*Titus Andronicus* [Act III, sc. 3]

BROOM

IRIS

And thy BROOM groves,
Whose shadow the dismissed bachelor loves,
Being lass-lorn.

—Tempest [Act IV, sc. 1]

PUCK

I am sent with BROOM* before
To sweep the dust behind the door.

—A Midsummer Night's Dream [Act V, sc. 1]

JAILER'S DAUGHTER

Yes, truly can I. I can sing The BROOM
and Bonny Robin. Are not you a tailor?

—Two Noble Kinsmen [Act IV, sc. 1]

BURDOCK

CORDELIA

Crown'd with rank fumiter and furrow-weeds,
With *BURDOCKS, hemlocke,
nettles, cuckoo-flowres
Darnell, and all the idle weeds that grow
in our sustaining corn.

—*King Lear* [Act IV, sc. 4]

BURGUNDY

And nothing teems
But hateful docks, rough thistles,
kecksies, BURS.

—*Henry V* [Act V, sc. 2]

CELIA

They are but BURS, cousin,
thrown upon thee in holiday foolery;
if we walk not in the trodden paths
our very petticoats will catch them.

ROSALIND

I could shake them off of my coat;
these BURS are in my heart.

—*As You Like It* [Act I, sc. 3]

LUCIO

Nay, friar, I am a kind of BUR; I shall stick.

—*Measure for Measure* [Act IV, sc. 3]

LYSANDER

Hang off, thou cat, thou BURR.

—*A Midsummer Night's Dream* [Act III, sc. 2]

PANDARUS

They are BURS, I can tell you;
they'll stick where they are thrown.

—*Troilus and Cressida* [Act III, sc. 2]

BURNET

BURGUNDY

The even mead, that erst brought sweetly forth
The freckled cowslip, BURNET,
and green clover . . .

—*Henry V* [Act V, sc. 2]

CABBAGE

SIR HUGH EVANS

Pauca verba, Sir John; good worts.

FALSTAFF

Good worts?! Good CABBAGE.

—*Merry Wives of Windsor* [Act I, sc. 1]

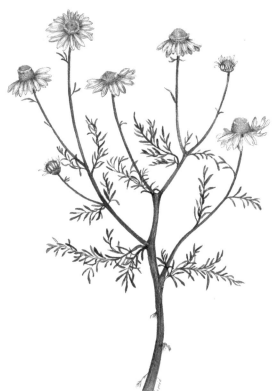

CAMOMILE

FALSTAFF

Though the CAMOMILE,
the more it is trodden,
the faster it grows;
yet youth, the more it is wasted,
the sooner it wears.

—*Henry IV, Pt.* 1 [Act II, sc. 4]

CAPER

SIR ANDREW AGUECHEEK
Faith, I can cut a CAPER.

SIR TOBY BELCH
And I can cut the mutton to't.

SIR ANDREW AGUECHEEK
... Shall we set about some revels?...

SIR TOBY BELCH
No, sir; it is legs and thighs. Let me see the
CAPER; ha! Higher: ha, ha! Excellent!

—*Twelfth Night* [Act I, sc. 3]

CARDUUS BENEDICTUS

Holy Thistle

MARGARET

Get you some of this distilled CARDUUS
BENEDICTUS, and lay it to your heart;
it is the only thing for a qualm.

HERO

There thou prickest her with a THISTLE.

BEATRICE

BENEDICTUS! Why BENEDICTUS? You
have some moral in this
BENEDICTUS.

MARGARET

Moral! No, by my troth, I have
no moral meaning: I meant plain
HOLY THISTLE.

—*Much Ado About Nothing* [Act III, sc. 4]

CARNATIONS

*Gillyvors*Pinks*

PERDITA

The fairest flowers o' the season
Are our CARNATIONS and streak'd GILLYVORS,
Which some call Nature's bastards.

—*Winter's Tale* [Act IV, sc. 4]

POLIXENES

Then make your garden rich in GILLYVORS,
And do not call them bastards.

—Winter's Tale [Act IV, sc. 4]

HOSTESS / MISTRESS QUICKLY

'A could never abide CARNATION;
'twas a colour he never liked.

—Henry V [Act II, sc. 3]

COSTARD

Pray you, sir, how much CARNATION ribbon
may a man buy for a remuneration?

—Love's Labour's Lost [Act III, sc. 1]

ROMEO

A most courteous exposition.

MERCUTIO

Nay, I am the very PINK of courtesy.

ROMEO

PINK for flower?

MERCUTIO

Right.

ROMEO

Why, then is my pump well flowered.

—Romeo and Juliet [Act II, sc. 4]

SONG [BOY]

Maiden PINKS of odour faint.

—Two Noble Kinsmen [Act I, sc. 1]

CARRAWAY

*Carrawayes*Carroway*
Leather-coats

SHALLOW

Nay, you shall see my orchard, where in an arbour
we will eat a last year's pippin of my own graffing,
with a dish of CARRAWAYES and so forth.

—*Henry IV, Pt. 2* [Act V, sc. 3]

DAVY

There's a dish of LEATHER-COATS for you.

—*Henry IV, Pt. 2* [Act V, sc. 3]

CARROT

Caret

SIR HUGH EVANS

Remember, William, focative is CARET.

MISTRESS QUICKLY

And that's a GOOD ROOT.

—*Merry Wives of Windsor* [Act IV, sc. 1]

CEDAR

PROSPERO

And by the spurs pluck'd up
The pine and CEDAR.

—*Tempest* [Act V, sc. 1]

WARWICK

As on a mountain top the CEDAR shows,
That keeps his leaves in spite of any storm.

—*Henry IV*, *Pt.* 2 [Act V, sc. 1]

WARWICK

Thus yields the CEDAR to the axe's edge,
Whose arms gave shelter to the princely eagle,
Under whose shade the ramping lion slept,
Whose top-branch o'erpeered Jove's spreading tree,
And kept low shrubs from winter's powerful wind.

—*Henry IV, Pt. 3* [Act V, sc. 2]

CRANMER

He shall flourish,
And, like a mountain CEDAR,
reach his branches
To all the plains about him.

—*Henry VIII* [Act V, sc. 5]

POSTHUMUS

When from a stately CEDAR shall be lopped
branches, which, being dead many years,
shall after revive.

—*Cymbeline* [Act V, sc. 4]

SOOTHSAYER

The lofty CEDAR, royal Cymbeline,
Personates thee. Thy lopp'd branches
Thy two sons forth; who, by Belarius stol'n,
For many years thought dead are now revived,
To the majestic CEDAR join'd whose issue
Promises Britain peace and plenty.

—*Cymbeline* [Act V, sc. 5]

DUMAIN

As upright as the CEDAR.

—*Love's Labour's Lost* [Act IV, sc. 3]

GLOUCESTER

But I was born so high,
Our aery buildeth in the CEDAR'S top,
And dallies with the wind and scorns the sun.

—*Richard III* [Act I, sc. 3]

CORIOLANUS

Let the mutinous winds
Strike the proud CEDARS
'gainst the fiery sun.

—*Coriolanus* [Act V, sc. 3]

TITUS

Marcus, we are but shrubs, no CEDARS we.

—*Titus Andronicus* [Act IV, sc. 3]

JAILER'S DAUGHTER

I have sent him where a CEDAR,
Higher than all the rest, spreads like a plane
Fast by a brook.

—*Two Noble Kinsmen* [Act II, sc. 6]

The sun ariseth in his majesty;
Who doth the world so gloriously behold
That CEDAR-tops and hills seem burnished
by gold.

—*Venus and Adonis*

The CEDAR stoops not to the base shrub's foot,
But low shrubs wither at the CEDAR's root.

—*Lucrece*

CHERRY

HELENA

So we grew together,
Like to a DOUBLE CHERRY, seeming parted,
But yet a union in partition;
Two lovely berries moulded on one stem.

—*A Midsummer Night's Dream* [Act III, sc. 2]

OLD LADY

'Tis as like you
As CHERRY is to CHERRY.

—*Henry VIII* [Act V, sc. 1]

FIRST QUEEN

Oh, when
Her twinning CHERRIES
shall their sweetness fall
Upon thy tasteful lips . . .

—*Two Noble Kinsmen* [Act I, sc. 1]

DEMETRIUS

O, how ripe in show
Thy lips, those kissing CHERRIES,
tempting grow!

—*A Midsummer Night's Dream* [Act III, sc. 2]

THISBE

My CHERRY lips have often kiss'd thy stones,
Thy stones with lime and hair knit up in thee.

—*A Midsummer Night's Dream* [Act V, sc. 1]

GLOUCESTER

We say that Shore's wife hath a pretty foot,
A CHERRY lip, a bonny eye,
a passing pleasing tongue.

—*Richard III* [Act I, sc. 1]

THISBE

These my lips
This CHERRY nose,
These yellow cowslip cheeks,
Are gone, are gone . . .

—*A Midsummer Night's Dream* [Act V, sc. 1]

CONSTANCE

Give it a plum, a CHERRY, and a fig.

—*King John* [Act II, sc. 1]

WOOER

I'll bring a bevy,
A hundred black-eyed maids that love as I do,
With chaplets on their heads of daffadillies,
With CHERRY lips and cheeks
of damask roses . . .

—*Two Noble Kinsmen* [Act IV, sc. 1]

DROMIO OF SYRACUSE

Some devils ask but the paring of one's nail,
A rush, a hair, a drop of blood, a pin,
A nut, a CHERRY-STONE.

—*Comedy of Errors* [Act IV, sc. 3]

SIR TOBY BELCH

What, man! 'tis not for
gravity to play at CHERRY-PIT with Satan:
hang him, foul collier!

—*Twelfth Night* [Act III, sc. 4]

GOWER

She with her needle composes
Nature's own shape of bud, bird, branch, or berry;
That even her art sisters, natural roses,
Her inkle, silk, twin with the rubied CHERRY.

—*Pericles* [Act IV, sc. 6]

When he was by, the birds such pleasure took,
That some would sing, some other in their bills
Would bring him mulberries
and ripe-red CHERRIES.
He fed them with his sight, they him with berries.

—*Venus and Adonis*

CHESTNUT

FIRST WITCH

A sailor's wife had CHESTNUTS
in her lap,
And munch'd, and munch'd,
and munch'd.

—*Macbeth* [Act I, sc. 3]

PETRUCHIO

And do you tell me of
a woman's tongue
That gives not half so great a blow to hear
As will a CHESTNUT
in a farmer's fire?

—*Taming of the Shrew* [Act I, sc. 2]

ROSALIND

I' faith, his hair is of a good colour.

CELIA

An excellent colour: your CHESTNUT
was ever the only colour.

—*As You Like It* [Act III, sc. 4]

CLOVER

BURGUNDY

The even mead, that erst brought sweetly forth
The freckled cowslip, burnet,
and green CLOVER.

—*Henry V* [Act V, sc. 2]

CLOVE

BIRON

A lemon.

LONGAVILLE

Stuck with CLOVES.

—*Love's Labour's Lost* [Act V, sc. 2]

COCKLE

BIRON

Allons! allons! Sowed COCKLE, reap'd no corn.

—*Love's Labour's Lost* [Act IV, sc. 3]

CORIOLANUS

We nourish 'gainst our senate
The COCKLE of rebellion, insolence, sedition,
Which we ourselves have plough'd for,
sow'd for, and scatter'd
By mingling them with us . . .

—*Coriolanus* [Act III, sc. 1]

JAILER'S DAUGHTER

There is at least two hundred now with child
by him—there must be four;
yet I keep close for all this, close as a COCKLE.

—*Two Noble Kinsmen* [Act IV, sc. 1]

OPHELIA [SINGS]

How should I your true love know
From another one?
By his COCKLE hat and staff,
And his sandal shoon.

—*Hamlet* [Act IV, sc. 5]

COLOQUINTIDA

IAGO

The food that to him now
is as luscious as locusts,
shall be to him shortly
as bitter as COLOQUINTIDA.

—*Othello* [Act I, sc. 3]

COLUMBINE

ARMANDO

I am that flower—

DUMAIN

That mint.

LONGAVILLE

That COLUMBINE.

—*Love's Labour's Lost* [Act V, sc. 2]

OPHELIA

There's fennel for you and COLUMBINES.

—*Hamlet* [Act IV, sc. 5]

CORK

ROSALIND

I prithee take the CORK out of thy mouth,
that I may hear thy tidings.

—*As You Like It* [Act III, sc. 2]

SHEPHERD'S SON / CLOWN

As you'ld thrust a CORK into a hogshead.

—*Winter's Tale* [Act III, sc. 3]

CORNWALL

Bind fast his CORKY arms.

—*King Lear* [Act III, sc. 7]

CORN

GONZALO

No use of metal, CORN, or wine, or oil.

—Tempest [Act II, sc. 1]

DUKE VINCENTIO

Our CORN'S to reap,

for yet our tithe's to sow.

—Measure for Measure [Act IV, sc. I]

TITANIA

... And in the shape of Corin sat all day,

Playing on pipes of CORN and versing love

To amorous Phillida.

—A Midsummer Night's Dream [Act II, sc. 1]

TITANIA

The ploughman lost his sweat,

and the green CORN

Hath rotted ere his youth attain'd a beard;

—A Midsummer Night's Dream [Act II, sc. 1]

EDWARD IV

What valiant foemen, like to autumn's CORN,

Have we mowed down in tops of all their pride!

—Henry VI, Pt. 3 [Act V, sc. 7]

SONG
[FIRST / SECOND PAGE]

That o'er the green CORN-FIELD did pass

In the spring time,

the only pretty ring time ...

—As You Like It [Act V, sc. 3]

JOAN LA PUCELLE

Talk like the vulgar sort of market men

That come to gather money for their CORN.

—Henry VI, Pt. 1 [Act III, sc. 2]

JOAN LA PUCELLE

Poor market folks that come to sell their CORN.

—Henry VI, Pt. 1 [Act III, sc. 2]

JOAN LA PUCELLE

Good morrow, gallants!

want ye CORN for bread?

—Henry VI, Pt. 1 [Act III, sc. 2]

BURGUNDY

I trust, ere long, to choke thee with thine own,

And make thee curse the harvest of that CORN.

—Henry VI, Pt. 1 [Act III, sc. 2]

DUCHESS OF GLOUCESTER / ELEANOR

Why droops my lord like over-ripened CORN
Hanging the head at Ceres' plenteous load?

—*Henry VI, Pt.* 2 [Act I, sc. 2]

WARWICK

His well-proportioned beard
made rough and ragged
Like to the summer's CORN by tempest lodged.

—*Henry VI, Pt.* 2 [Act III, sc. 2]

MOWBRAY

We shall be winnow'd with so rough a wind
That even our CORN
shall seem as light as chaff.

—*Henry IV, Pt.* 2 [Act IV, sc. 1]

MACBETH

Though bladed CORN be lodged and trees
blown down.

—*Macbeth* [Act IV, sc. 1]

LONGAVILLE

He weeds the CORN,
and still lets grow the weeding.

—*Love's Labour's Lost* [Act I, sc. 1]

BIRON

Allons! allons! sowed cockle, reap'd no CORN.

—*Love's Labour's Lost* [Act IV, sc. 3]

EDGAR

Sleepest or wakest thou, jolly shepherd?
Thy sheep be in the CORN.

—*King Lear* [Act III, sc. 6]

CORDELIA

All the idle weeds that grow
In our sustaining CORN.

—*King Lear* [Act IV, sc. 4]

DEMETRIUS

First thrash the CORN,
then after burn the straw.

—Titus Andronicus [Act II, sc. 3]

MARCUS

O, let me teach you how to knit again
This scattered CORN into one mutual sheaf.

—Titus Andronicus [Act V, sc. 3]

PERICLES

Our ships . . . are stored with CORN
to make your needy bread.

—Pericles [Act I, sc. 4]

CLEON

Your grace, that fed my country
with your CORN.

—Pericles [Act III, sc. 3]

FIRST CITIZEN

Let us kill him, and we'll have CORN
at our own price. Is't a verdict?

—Coriolanus [Act I, sc. 1]

MENENIUS

For CORN at their own rates.

—Coriolanus [Act I, sc. 1]

MARCIUS

The gods sent not CORN
for the rich men only.

—Coriolanus [Act I, sc. 1]

MARCIUS

The Volsces have much CORN.

—Coriolanus [Act I, sc. 1]

FIRST CITIZEN

For once we stood up about the CORN.

—Coriolanus [Act II, sc. 3]

BRUTUS

CORN was given them gratis.

—Coriolanus [Act III, sc. 1]

CORIOLANUS

Tell me of CORN!

—*Coriolanus* [Act III, sc. 1]

CORIOLANUS

Give forth
The CORN o' the storehouse gratis,
as 'twas used
Sometime in Greece.

—*Coriolanus* [Act III, sc. 1]

CORIOLANUS

They know the CORN
Was not our recompense, ...
This kind of service
Did not deserve CORN gratis.

—*Coriolanus* [Act III, sc. 1]

CRANMER

I am right glad to catch this good occasion
Most thoroughly to be winnow'd, where my chaff
And CORN shall fly asunder.

—*Henry VIII* [Act V, sc. 1]

CRANMER

Her foes shake like a field of beaten CORN
And hang their heads with sorrow.

—*Henry VIII* [Act V, sc. 5]

RICHARD II

We'll make foul weather with despised tears;
Our sighs and they shall lodge
the summer CORN.

—*Richard II* [Act III, sc. 3]

ARCITE

And run
Swifter than wind upon a field of CORN
Curling the wealthy ears ...

—*Two Noble Kinsmen* [Act II, sc. 3]

As CORN o'ergrown by weeds, so heedful fear
Is almost choked by unresisted lust.

—*Lucrece*

COWSLIP

BURGUNDY

The even mead, that erst brought sweetly forth
The freckled COWSLIP, burnet,
and green clover.

—Henry V [Act V, sc. 2]

QUEEN

The violets, COWSLIPS, and the primroses,
Bear to my closet.

—Cymbeline [Act I, sc. 5]

IACHIMO

On her left breast,
A mole, cinque-spotted, like the crimson drops
I' the bottom of a COWSLIP.

—Cymbeline [Act II, sc. 2]

ARIEL

Where the bee sucks there suck I,
In a COWSLIP'S bell I lie.

—Tempest [Act V, sc. 1]

FLUTE / THISBE

Those yellow COWSLIP cheeks.

—A Midsummer Night's Dream [Act V, sc. 1]

FAIRY

The COWSLIPS tall her pensioners be;
In their gold coats spots you see;
Those be rubies, fairy favours,
In those freckles live their saviours;
I must go seek some dewdrops here,
And hang a pearl in every COWSLIP'S ear.

—A Midsummer Night's Dream [Act II, sc. 1]

CRAB-APPLE

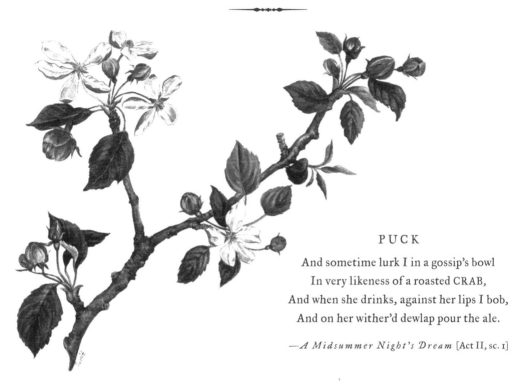

PUCK

And sometime lurk I in a gossip's bowl
In very likeness of a roasted CRAB,
And when she drinks, against her lips I bob,
And on her wither'd dewlap pour the ale.

—*A Midsummer Night's Dream* [Act II, sc. 1]

MENENIUS

We have some old CRAB-TREES here at home
that will not be grafted to your relish.

—*Coriolanus* [Act II, sc. 1]

SUFFOLK

And noble stock
Was graft with CRAB-TREE slip,
whose fruit thou art . . .

—*Henry VI, Pt. 2* [Act III, sc. 2]

SONG OF WINTER

When roasted CRABS hiss in the bowl,
Then nightly sings the starting owl.

—*Love's Labour's Lost* [Act V, sc. 2]

FOOL

Shalt see thy other daughter will use thee kindly;
for though she's as like this as a CRAB'S like
an APPLE, yet I can tell what I can tell.

LEAR

What canst thou tell, Boy?

FOOL

She will taste as like this
as a CRAB does to a CRAB.

—*King Lear* [Act I, sc. 5]

CALIBAN

I prithee, let me bring thee where CRABS grow.

—*Tempest* [Act II, sc. 2]

PORTER

Fetch me a dozen CRAB-TREE staves,
and strong ones.

—*Henry VIII* [Act V, sc. 4]

PETRUCHIO

Nay, come, Kate, come, you must not look so sour.

KATHERINE

It is my fashion, when I see a CRAB.

PETRUCHIO

Why, here's no CRAB, and therefore
look not sour.

—*Taming of the Shrew* [Act II, sc. 1]

HOLOFERNES / PEDANT

And anon falleth
like a CRAB on the face of *terra*—
the soil, the land, the earth.

—*Love's Labour's Lost* [Act IV, sc. 2]

CROW-FLOWERS

GERTRUDE

There with fantastic garlands
did she come
Of CROW-FLOWERS, nettles,
daisies, and long purples.

—*Hamlet* [Act IV, sc. 7]

CROWN IMPERIAL

PERDITA

Bold oxlips, and
The CROWN IMPERIAL.

—*Winter's Tale* [Act IV, sc. 4]

CUCKOO-BUDS

SONG OF SPRING

When daisies pied, and violets blue,
And lady-smocks all silver-white,
And CUCKOO-BUDS of yellow hue,
Do paint the meadows with delight.

—*Love's Labour's Lost* [Act V, sc. 2]

CURRANTS

SHEPHERD'S SON / CLOWN

What am I to buy for our sheep-shearing feast?
Three pound of sugar,
five pound of CURRANTS.

—*Winter's Tale* [Act IV, sc. 3]

THESEUS

I stamp this kiss upon thy CURRANT lip.

—*Two Noble Kinsmen* [Act I, sc. 1]

CYME

Senna

MACBETH

What rhubarb, CYME, or what purgative drug
Would scour these English hence?

—*Macbeth* [Act V, sc. 3]

CYPRESS

Cyprus

SUFFOLK

Their sweetest shade
a grove of CYPRESS trees!

—*Henry VI, Pt.* 2 [Act III, sc. 2]

SONG [FESTE]

In sad CYPRESS let me be laid.

—*Twelfth Night* [Act II, sc. 4]

OLIVIA

To one of your receiving
Enough is shown; a CYPRESS, not a bosom,
Hides my heart.

—*Twelfth Night* [Act III, sc. 1]

AUTOLYCUS

Lawn as white as driven snow,
CYPRUS, black as e'er was crow . . .

—*Winter's Tale* [Act IV, sc. 4]

AUFIDIUS

I am attended at the CYPRESS grove.

—*Coriolanus* [Act I, sc. 10]

GREMIO

In ivory coffers I have stuff'd my crowns,
In CYPRESS chests
are my arras counterpoints.

—*Taming of the Shrew* [Act II, sc. 1]

DAFFODIL

Narcissus

PERDITA

DAFFODILS
That come before the
swallow dares, and take
The winds of March
with beauty.

—*Winter's Tale* [Act IV, sc. 4]

WOOER

With chaplets on their heads
of DAFFADILLIES...

—*Two Noble Kinsmen* [Act IV, sc. 1]

EMILIA

This garden has a world of pleasures in't,
What flowre is this?

WOMAN

'Tis called NARCISSUS, madam.

EMILIA

That was a faire boy certaine,
but a foole
To love himself;
were there not maides enough?

—*Two Noble Kinsmen* [Act II, sc. 2]

AUTOLYCUS

When DAFFODILS begin to peer
With heigh! the doxy o'er the dale,
Why, then comes in the sweet o' the year.

—*Winter's Tale* [Act IV, sc. 3]

DAISIES

SONG OF SPRING

When DAISIES pied, and violets blue,
And lady-smocks all silver-white . . .

—*Love's Labour's Lost* [Act V, sc. 2]

OPHELIA

There's a DAISY.

—*Hamlet* [Act IV, sc. 5]

GERTRUDE

There with fantastic garlands did she come
Of crow-flowers, nettles, DAISIES,
and long purples . . .

—*Hamlet* [Act IV, sc. 7]

LUCIUS

Let us
Find out the prettiest DAISIED plot we can,
And make him, with our pikes and partizans,
A grave.

—*Cymbeline* [Act IV, sc. 2]

Her other faire hand was
On the green coverlet, whose perfect white
Show'd like an APRIL DAISY
on the grass . . .

—*Lucrece*

SONG [BOY]

DAISIES, smell-less yet most quaint . . .

—*Two Noble Kinsmen* [Act I, sc. 1]

DARNEL

CORDELIA

DARNEL, and all the idle weeds that grow
In our sustaining corn.

—*King Lear* [Act IV, sc. 4]

BURGUNDY

Her fallow leas,
The DARNEL,
hemlock and rank fumitory
Doth root upon.

—*Henry V* [Act V, sc. 2]

JOAN LA PUCELLE

Want ye corn for bread?
I think the Duke of Burgundy will fast
Before he'll buy again at such a rate;
'Twas full of DARNEL—do you like the taste?

—*Henry VI, Pt. 1* [Act III, sc. 2]

DATES

SHEPHERD'S SON / CLOWN

I must have saffron to colour the warden pies—
Mace; DATES? None; that's out of my note.

—*Winter's Tale* [Act IV, sc. 3]

NURSE

They call for DATES and quinces
in the pastry.

—*Romeo and Juliet* [Act IV, sc. 4]

PAROLLES

Your DATE is better in your pie and your
porridge than in your cheek.

—*All's Well That Ends Well* [Act I, sc. 1]

PANDARUS

Do you know what a man is?
Is not birth, beauty, good shape, discourse,
manhood, learning, gentleness, virtue,
youth, liberality, and suchlike,
the spice and salt that season a man?

CRESSIDA

Ay, a minced man;
and then to be baked with no DATE in the pie;
for then the man's DATE'S out.

—*Troilus and Cressida* [Act I, sc. 2]

DEWBERRIES

TITANIA

Feed him with apricocks and
DEWBERRIES.

—*A Midsummer Night's Dream* [Act III, sc. 1]

DOCKS

BURGUNDY

And nothing teems
But hateful DOCKS, rough thistles,
kecksies, burs.

—*Henry V* [Act V, sc. 2]

EBONY

KING FERDINAND

By heaven, thy love is black as EBONY.

BIRON

Is EBONY like her? O wood divine!
A wife of such wood were felicity.

—*Love's Labour's Lost* [Act IV, sc. 3]

FESTE / CLOWN

The clearstores towards the south north
are as lustrous as EBONY.

—*Twelfth Night* [Act IV, sc. 2]

PISTOL

Rouse up revenge from EBON den with fell
Alecto's snake ...

—*Henry IV, Pt.* 2 [Act V, sc. 5]

KING FERDINAND

The EBON-COLOURED ink.

—*Love's Labour's Lost* [Act I, sc. 1]

Love's golden arrow at him should have fled,
And not Death's EBON dart, to strike dead.

—*Venus and Adonis*

EGLANTINE

ARVIRAGUS

Thou shalt not lack
The flower that's like thy face, pale primrose, nor
The azured harebell like thy veins, no, nor
The leaf of EGLANTINE,
whom not to slander,
Out-sweeten'd not thy breath.

—*Cymbeline* [Act IV, sc. 2]

OBERON

I know a bank where the wild thyme blows,
Where oxlips and the nodding violet grows
Quite over-canopied with luscious woodbine,
With sweet musk-roses
and with EGLANTINE.

—*A Midsummer Night's Dream* [Act II, sc. 1]

ELDER

ARVIRAGUS

And let the stinking ELDER, grief, untwine
His perishing root with the increasing vine!

—*Cymbeline* [Act IV, sc. 2]

SATURNINUS

"Look for thy reward
Among the nettles at the ELDER-TREE
Which overshades the mouth of that same pit
Where we decreed to bury Bassianus.
Do this, and purchase us thy lasting friends."
O Tamora! Was ever heard the like?
This is the pit, and this the ELDER-TREE.

—*Titus Andronicus* [Act II, sc. 3]

HOLOFERNES / PEDANT

Begin, sir, you are my ELDER.

BIRON

Well followed; Judas was hanged on an ELDER.

—*Love's Labour's Lost* [Act V, sc. 2]

WILLIAMS

That's a perilous shot
out of an ELDER gun,
that a poor and private displeasure
can do against a monarch.

—*Henry V* [Act IV, sc. 1]

PRINCE HENRY

Look, whether the withered ELDER
hath not his poll clawed like a parrot.

—*Henry IV, Pt. 2* [Act II, sc. 4]

HOST OF THE GARTER

What says my Aesculapius? my Galen?
my heart of ELDER?

—*Merry Wives of Windsor* [Act II, sc. 3]

ELM

ADRIANA

Thou art an ELM, my husband, I a vine,
Whose weakness married to thy stronger state
Makes me with thy strength to communicate.

—Comedy of Errors [Act II, sc. 2]

TITANIA

The female ivy so
Enrings the barky fingers of the ELM.

—A Midsummer Night's Dream [Act IV, sc. 1]

POINS

Answer, thou dead ELM, answer!

—Henry IV, Pt. 2 [Act II, sc. 4]

ERINGOES

FALSTAFF

Let the sky rain potatoes;
let it thunder to the tune
of Greensleeves, hail kissing-comfits,
and snow ERINGOES.

—*Merry Wives of Windsor* [Act V, sc. 5]

FENNEL

OPHELIA

There's FENNEL for you and columbines.

—*Hamlet* [Act IV, sc. 5]

FALSTAFF

Because their legs are both of a bigness,
and a' plays at quoits well,
and eats conger and FENNEL...

—*Henry IV, Pt. 2* [Act II, sc. 4]

FERN

Fern-Seed

GADSHILL

We have the receipt of FERN-SEED—
we walk invisible.

CHAMBERLAIN

Now, by my faith, I think you are
more beholding to the night
than to FERN-SEED
for your walking invisible.

—*Henry IV, Pt.* I [Act II, sc. I]

FIG

TITANIA

Feed him with apricocks
and dewberries,
With purple grapes, green FIGS,
and mulberries.

—*A Midsummer Night's Dream* [Act III, sc. I]

CONSTANCE

And its grandam will
Give it a plum, a cherry, and a FIG.

—*King John* [Act II, sc. I]

FIRST GUARD

Here is a rural fellow
That will not be denied your Highness's presence,
He brings you FIGS.

—*Antony and Cleopatra* [Act V, sc. 2]

FIRST GUARD

A simple countryman that brought her FIGS.

—*Antony and Cleopatra* [Act V, sc. 2]

FIRST GUARD

These FIG-LEAVES
Have slime upon them.

—*Antony and Cleopatra* [Act V, sc. 2]

PISTOL

When Pistol lies, do this; and FIG me, like
The bragging Spaniard.

—*Henry IV, Pt. 2* [Act V, sc. 3]

PISTOL

Die and be damned,
and FIGO for thy friendship.

FLUELLEN

It is well.

PISTOL

The FIG of Spain.

—*Henry V* [Act III, sc. 6]

PISTOL

The FIGO for thee, then.

—*Henry V* [Act IV, sc. 1]

PISTOL

"Convey," the wise it call. "Steal?"
foh! a FICO for the phrase!

—*Merry Wives of Windsor* [Act I, sc. 3]

IAGO

Virtue! a FIG!

—*Othello* [Act I, sc. 3]

IAGO

Blessed FIG's end!

—*Othello* [Act II, sc. 1]

HORNER

I'll pledge you all, and a FIG for Peter.

—*Henry VI, Pt. 2* [Act II, sc. 3]

CHARMIAN

O excellent! I love long life better than FIGS.

—*Antony and Cleopatra* [Act I, sc. 2]

FLAGS

OCTAVIUS CÆSAR

This common body
Like to a vagabond FLAG upon the stream
Goes to and back, lackeying the varying tide,
To root itself with motion.

—Antony and Cleopatra [Act I, sc. 4]

FLAX

FORD

What, a hodge-pudding? a bag of FLAX?

—*Merry Wives of Windsor* [Act V, sc. 5]

CLIFFORD

Beauty that the tyrant oft reclaims
Shall to my flaming wrath be oil and FLAX.

—*Henry VI, Pt. 2* [Act V, sc. 2]

SIR TOBY BELCH

Excellent; it hangs like FLAX on a distaff.

—*Twelfth Night* [Act I, sc. 3]

THIRD SERVANT

Go thou; I'll fetch some FLAX
and white of eggs
To apply to his bleeding face.

—*King Lear* [Act III, sc. 7]

OPHELIA

His beard was as white as snow,
All FLAXEN was his poll.

—*Hamlet* [Act IV, sc. 5]

LEONTES

My wife deserves a name.
As rank as any FLAX-WENCH.

—*Winter's Tale* [Act I, sc. 2]

EMILIA

It could
No more be hid in him than fire in FLAX.

—*Two Noble Kinsmen* [Act V, sc. 3]

FLOWER-DE-LUCE

Fleur-de-lis

HENRY V

What sayest thou, my fair
FLOWER-DE-LUCE?

—*Henry V* [Act V, sc. 2]

MESSENGER

Cropped are the FLOWER-
DE-LUCES
in your arms;
Of England's coat one half is cut away.

—*Henry VI, Pt. 1* [Act I, sc. 1]

JOAN LA PUCELLE

I am prepared; here is my keen-edged sword
Deck'd with five FLOWER-DE-LUCES
on each side.

—*Henry VI, Pt. 1* [Act I, sc. 2]

YORK

A sceptre shall it have, have I a soul,
On which I'll toss the FLOWER-
DE-LUCE of France.

—*Henry VI, Pt. 2* [Act V, sc. 1]

PERDITA

Lilies of all kinds,
The FLOWER-DE-LUCE being one.

—*Winter's Tale* [Act IV, sc. 4]

FUMITER

*Fumitory*Fenitar*Furrow-weeds*

CORDELIA

Crown'd with rank FUMITER and
FURROW-WEEDS.

—*King Lear* [Act IV, sc. 4]

BURGUNDY

Her fallow leas
The darnel, hemlock,
and rank FUMITORY
Doth root upon.

—*Henry V* [Act V, sc. 2]

FURZE

*Goss*Gorse*

ARIEL

So I charm'd their ears,
That calf-like they my lowing follow'd, through
Tooth'd briers, sharp FURZES, pricking
GOSS and thorns
Which entered their frail shins.

—*Tempest* [Act IV, sc. 1]

GONZALO

Now would I give a thousand furlongs of sea for
an acre of barren ground, long* heath,
brown FURZE, anything.

—*Tempest* [Act I, sc. 1]

GARLIC

*Garlick*Garlicke*

BOTTOM

Most dear Actors, eat no onions
nor GARLICKE,
for we are to utter sweet breath.

—*A Midsummer Night's Dream* [Act IV, sc. 2]

LUCIO

He would mouth with a beggar,
though she smelt brown bread
and GARLICKE.

—*Measure for Measure* [Act III, sc. 2]

HOTSPUR

I had rather live,
With cheese and GARLICK in a windmill.

—*Henry IV, Pt. 1* [Act III, sc. 1]

MENENIUS

You that stood so up much
On the voice of occupation, and
The breath of GARLIC-EATERS.

—*Coriolanus* [Act IV, sc. 6]

DORCAS

Mopsa must be your mistress; marry,
GARLICK to mend her kissing with.

—*Winter's Tale* [Act IV, sc. 4]

GINGER

SHEPHERD'S SON / CLOWN

Mace, Dates? None, that's out of my note;
Nutmegs, seven—a race or two of GINGER,
but that I may beg.

—Winter's Tale [Act IV, sc. 3]

FESTE / CLOWN

Yes, by St. Anne, and GINGER
shall be hot i' the mouth too.

—Twelfth Night [Act II, sc. 3]

POMPEY

First, here's Young Master Rash, he's in for a
commodity of brown paper and old GINGER,
nine score and seventeen pounds,
of which he made five marks ready money;
marry, then, GINGER was not much
in request, for the old women were all dead.

—Measure for Measure [Act IV, sc. 3]

SECOND CARRIER

I have a gammon of bacon and two razes
of GINGER to be delivered
as far as Charing Cross.

—Henry IV, Pt. 1 [Act II, sc. 1]

SALANIO

I would she were as lying a gossip in that
as ever knapped GINGER.

—Merchant of Venice [Act III, sc. 1]

ORLEANS

He's of the colour of the nutmeg.

DAUPHIN

And of the heat of the GINGER.

—Henry V [Act III, sc. 7]

GOOSEBERRY

FALSTAFF

All of the other gifts appertinent to man,
as the malice of this age shapes them,
are not worth a GOOSEBERRY.

—Henry IV, Pt. 2 [Act I, sc. 2]

MACBETH

The devil damn thee black,
thou cream-faced loon!
Where got'st thou that GOOSE look?

—Macbeth [Act V, sc. 3]

BIRON

This is the liver-vein, which makes flesh a deity,
a GREEN GOOSE a goddess:
pure, pure idolatry.

—Love's Labour's Lost [Act IV, sc. 3]

GOURD

*Pumpion*Marrow*Curbita*

MISTRESS FORD

We'll use this unwholesome humidity,
this gross watery PUMPION.

—*Merry Wives of Windsor* [Act III, sc. 3]

TIMON

O, a root,—dear thanks!—
Dry up thy MARROWS, vines,
and plough-torn leas
Whereof ungrateful man, with liquorish draughts
And morsels unctuous, greases his pure mind,
That from it all consideration slips!

—*Timon of Athens*
[Act IV, sc. 3]

PAROLLES

A good knave, i' faith, and well fed....
Whose want, and whose delay,
is strew'd with sweets,
Which they distil now
in the CURBED TIME [CURBITA]
To make the coming hour o'erflow with joy
And pleasure drown the brim.

—*All's Well That Ends Well* [Act II, sc. 4]

PISTOL

For GOURD and fullam holds.

—*Merry Wives of Windsor* [Act I, sc. 3]

GRAPES

Raisins [*see also Vines**]

TITANIA

Feed him with apricocks and dewberries,
With purple GRAPES, green figs,
and mulberries.

—*A Midsummer Night's Dream* [Act III, sc. 1]

SONG

Come, thou monarch of the VINE,
Plumpy Bacchus, with pink eyne!
In thy fats our cares be drown'd,
With thy GRAPES our hairs be crown'd.

—*Antony and Cleopatra* [Act II, sc. 7]

CLEOPATRA

Now no more
The juice of Egypt's GRAPE shall moist this lip.

—*Antony and Cleopatra*
[Act V, sc. 2]

TIMON

Go, suck the subtle blood o' the GRAPE,
Till the high fever seethe your blood to froth.

—*Timon of Athens* [Act IV, sc. 3]

TOUCHSTONE

The heathen philosopher, when he had a desire
to eat a GRAPE, would open his lips when he
put it into his mouth; meaning thereby that
GRAPES were made to eat and lips to open.

—*As You Like It* [Act V, sc. 1]

MENENIUS

The tartness of his face sours ripe GRAPES.

—*Coriolanus* [Act V, sc. 4]

LAFEU

There's one GRAPE yet.

—*All's Well That Ends Well* [Act II, sc. 1]

IAGO

Blessed fig's end! the wine she drinks
is made of GRAPES.

—*Othello* [Act II, sc. 1]

LAFEU

O, will you eat no GRAPES, my royal fox?
Yes, but you will my noble GRAPES, an if
My royal fox could reach them.

—*All's Well That Ends Well* [Act II, sc. 1]

POMPEY

... 'twas in "The Bunch of GRAPES,"
where, indeed, you have a delight to sit.

—*Measure for Measure* [Act II, sc. 1]

PIRITHOUS

His complexion
Is, as a ripe GRAPE, ruddy.

—*Two Noble Kinsmen* [Act IV, sc. 2]

Even as poor birds,
deceived with painted GRAPES,
Do surfeit by the eye and pine the maw.

—*Venus and Adonis*

For one sweet GRAPE,
who will the VINE destroy?

—*Lucrece*

SHEPHERD'S SON / CLOWN

Four pound of prunes,
and as many of RAISINS O' THE SUN.

—*Winter's Tale* [Act IV, sc. 3]

GRASSES

*Stover*Fescue*Honey-stalks*

FIRST BANDIT

We cannot live on GRASS, on berries, water,
As beasts and birds and fishes.

—*Timon of Athens* [Act IV, sc. 3]

CERES

Why hath thy Queen
Summon'd me hither
to this SHORT-GRASS'D green?

—*Tempest* [Act IV, sc. 1]

ELY

Grew like the summer GRASS,
fastest by night . . .

—*Henry V* [Act I, sc. 1]

LAVATCH / CLOWN

I am no great Nebuchadnezzar, sir,
I have not much skill in GRASS.

—*All's Well That Ends Well* [Act IV, sc. 5]

HENRY V

Mowing like GRASS
Your fresh-fair virgins and your flowering infants.

—*Henry V* [Act III, sc. 3]

RICHARD II

And bedew
Her pasture's GRASS
with faithful English blood.

—*Richard II* [Act III, sc. 3]

GRANDPRE

And in their pale dull mouths the gimmal bit
Lies foul with chew'd GRASS,
still and motionless.

—*Henry V* [Act IV, sc. 2]

TAMORA

I will enchant the old Andronicus
With words more sweet, and yet more dangerous,
Than baits to fish,
or HONEY-STALKS to sheep,
When, as the one is wounded with the bait,
The other rotted with delicious feed.

—*Titus Andronicus* [Act IV, sc. 4]

IRIS

Thy turfy mountains, where live nibbling sheep,
and flat meads thatch'd with STOVER,
them to keep.

—*Tempest* [Act IV, sc. 1]

SUFFOLK

Though standing naked on a mountain top
Where biting cold would never let GRASS grow.

—*Henry VI, Pt. 2* [Act III, sc. 2]

LYSANDER

When Phœbe doth behold
Her silver visage in the watery glass,
Decking with liquid pearl the bladed GRASS.

—*A Midsummer Night's Dream* [Act I, sc. 1]

JOHN OF GAUNT

Suppose the singing birds musicians,
The GRASS whereon thou tread'st
the presence strew'd,
The flowers fair ladies.

—*Richard II* [Act I, sc. 3]

JACK CADE

All the realm shall be in common;
and in Cheapside shall my
palfrey go to GRASS.

—*Henry VI, Pt. 2* [Act IV, sc. 2]

JACK CADE

Wherefore on a brick wall have I climbed into
this garden, to see if I can eat GRASS or pick
a sallet another while, which is not amiss to
cool a man's stomach this hot weather.

—*Henry VI, Pt. 2* [Act IV, sc. 10]

KING FERDINAND

Say to her, we have measured many miles
To tread a measure with her on this GRASS.

BOYET

They say, that they have measured
many a mile
To tread a measure with you on the GRASS.

—*Love's Labour's Lost* [Act V, sc. 2]

SATURNINUS

These tidings nip me, and I hang the head
As flowers with frost or GRASS
beat down with storms.

—*Titus Andronicus* [Act IV, sc. 4]

HAMLET

Ay but, sir, "while the GRASS grows"—the
proverb is something musty.

—Hamlet [Act III, sc. 2]

OPHELIA

He is dead and gone, lady,
He is dead and gone;
At his head a GRASS-GREEN turf,
At his heels a stone.

—Hamlet [Act IV, sc. 5]

LUCIANA

If thou art changed to aught, 'tis to an ass.

DROMIO OF SYRACUSE

'Tis true; she rides me, and I long for GRASS.

—Comedy of Errors [Act II, sc. 2]

SALARINO

I should be still
Plucking the GRASS to know where sits
the wind.

—Merchant of Venice [Act I, sc. 1]

GONZALO

How lush and lusty the GRASS looks!
how green!

—Tempest [Act II, sc. 1]

IRIS

Here, on this GRASS-PLOT, in this very place
To come and sport.

—Tempest [Act IV, sc. 1]

BOLINGBROKE

Here we march
Upon the GRASSY carpet of the plain.

—Richard II [Act III, sc. 3]

THIRD COUNTRYMAN

Ay, do, but put
a FESCUE in her fist and you shall see her
take a new lesson out and be a good wench.
Do we all hold against the Maying?

—Two Noble Kinsmen [Act II, sc. 3]

Within this limit is relief enough,
Sweet BOTTOM-GRASS
and high delightful plain,
Round rising hillocks,
BRAKES obscure and rough . . .

—Venus and Adonis

The GRASS stoops not,
she treads on it so light.

—Venus and Adonis

For on the GRASS she lies as she were slain,
Till his breath breatheth life in her again.

—Venus and Adonis

HAREBELL

ARVIRAGUS

Thou shalt not lack
The flower that's like thy face, pale primrose, nor
The azured HAREBELL, like thy veins.

—*Cymbeline* [Act IV, sc. 2]

HAWTHORN

Hawthorn-buds*Brake*
Hawthorn-blossom*May Tree*

ROSALIND

There's a man . . . hangs odes upon
HAWTHORNS and elegies on brambles.

—*As You Like It* [Act III, sc. 2]

PETER QUINCE

This green plot shall be our stage, this
HAWTHORN-BRAKE our tiring house.

—*A Midsummer Night's Dream* [Act III, sc. 1]

PUCK

I'll lead you about a round,
Through bog, through bush, through BRAKE,
through brier.

—*A Midsummer Night's Dream* [Act III, sc. 1]

HELENA

Your tongue's sweet air,
More tuneable than lark to shepherd's ear,
When wheat is green, when
HAWTHORN-BUDS appear.

—*A Midsummer Night's Dream* [Act I, sc. 1]

FALSTAFF

I cannot cog and say thou art this and that,
like a many of these lisping HAWTHORN-BUDS
that come like women in men's apparel.

—*Merry Wives of Windsor* [Act III, sc. 3]

HENRY VI

Gives not the HAWTHORN-BUSH
a sweeter shade
to shepherds looking on their silly sheep,
Than doth a rich embroider'd canopy
To kings that fear their subjects' treachery?
O yes, it doth; a thousand-fold it doth.

—*Henry VI, Pt. 3* [Act II, sc. 5]

EDGAR

Through the sharp HAWTHORN
blows the cold wind.

—*King Lear* [Act III, sc. 4]

ARCITE

Again betake you to yon HAWTHORN house.

—*Two Noble Kinsmen* [Act III, sc. 1]

Rough winds do shake the
darling BUDS OF MAY,
And summer's lease hath all too short a date.

—*Sonnet XVIII*

HAMLET

He took my father grossly, full of bread,
With all his crimes broad blown, as flush as
MAY.

—*Hamlet* [Act III, sc. 3]

HAZEL / NUT

*Filberds*Filberts*Philbirtes*

MERCUTIO

Her chariot is an empty HAZEL-NUT
Made by the joiner squirrel or old grub,
Time out o' mind the fairies' coachmakers.

—*Romeo and Juliet* [Act I, sc. 4]

PETRUCHIO

Kate like the HAZEL twig
Is straight and slender and as brown in hue
As HAZEL-NUTS
and sweeter than the kernels.

—*Taming of the Shrew* [Act II, sc. 1]

MERCUTIO

Thou wilt quarrel with a man for cracking NUTS,
having no other reason but
because thou has HAZEL eyes.

—*Romeo and Juliet* [Act III, sc. 1]

THERSITES

Hector shall have a great catch,
if he knock out either of your brains;
a' were as good crack a fusty NUT with no kernel.

—*Troilus and Cressida* [Act II, sc. 1]

GONZALO

I'll warrant him for drowning; though the ship
were no stronger than a NUT-SHELL.

—*Tempest* [Act I, sc. 1]

CALIBAN

I'll bring three to clustering FILBERDS.

—*Tempest* [Act II, sc. 2]

TITANIA

I have a venturous fairy that shall seek
The squirrel's hoard, and fetch thee new NUTS.

—*A Midsummer Night's Dream* [Act IV, sc. 1]

TOUCHSTONE

Sweetest NUT hath sourest rind,
Such a NUT is Rosalind.

—*As You Like It* [Act III, sc. 2]

HAMLET

O God, I could be bounded in a NUT-SHELL and
count myself a king of infinite space,
were it not that I have bad dreams.

—*Hamlet* [Act II, sc. 2]

CELIA

For his verity in love I do think him as concave
as a covered goblet or a worm-eaten NUT.

—*As You Like It* [Act III, sc. 4]

DROMIO OF SYRACUSE

Some devils ask but the parings of one's nail,
A rush, a hair, a drop of blood, a pin,
A NUT, a cherry-stone.

—*Comedy of Errors* [Act IV, sc. 3]

LAFEU

Believe this of me,
there can be no kernel in this light NUT.

—*All's Well That Ends Well* [Act II, sc. 5]

HEATH

Ling

— ⟡ —

GONZALO

Now would I give a thousand furlongs of sea for an
acre of barren ground, long* HEATH,
brown furze, anything.

—*Tempest* [Act I, sc. 1]

[sometimes *ling]

HEBENON / HEBONA

*Yew*Deadly Nightshade*Hemlock*

— ⟡ —

GHOST

Upon my secure hour thy uncle stole,
With juice of cursed HEBENON in a vial,
And in the porches of my ear did pour
The leperous distilment; whose effect
Holds such an enmity with blood of man
That swift as quicksilver it courses through
The natural gates and alleys of the body,
And with a sudden vigour it doth posset
And curd, like eager droppings into milk,
The thin and wholesome blood; so did it mine;
And most instant tetter bark'd about,
Most Lazar-like, with vile and loathsome crust,
All my smooth body.

—*Hamlet* [Act I, sc. 5]

HEMLOCK

THIRD WITCH

Root of HEMLOCK digg'd i' the dark.

—*Macbeth* [Act IV, sc. 2]

BURGUNDY

Her fallow leas
The darnel, HEMLOCK,
and rank fumitory
Doth root upon.

—*Henry V* [Act V, sc. 2]

CORDELIA

Crown'd with rank fumiter and furrow-weeds,
With burdocks, HEMLOCK,
nettles, cuckoo-flowers.

—*King Lear* [Act IV, sc. 4]

HEMP

PISTOL

Let gallows gape for dog; let man go free,
And let not HEMP his windpipe suffocate.

—*Henry V* [Act III, sc. 6]

CHORUS

And in them behold
Upon the HEMPEN tackle ship-boys climbing.

—*Henry V* [Act III, Chorus]

JACK CADE

Ye shall have a HEMPEN caudle then,
and the pap of a hatchet.

—*Henry IV, Pt. 2* [Act IV, sc. 7]

PUCK

What HEMPEN homespuns
have we swaggering here?

—*A Midsummer Night's Dream* [Act III, sc. 1]

HOSTESS / MISTRESS QUICKLY

Thou HEMP-SEED.

—*Henry IV, Pt. 2* [Act II, sc. 1]

HOLLY

SONG [AMIENS]

Heigh-ho! sing heigh-ho! unto the green HOLLY:
Most friendship is feigning, most loving mere folly:
Then, heigh-ho, the HOLLY!
This life is most jolly.

—*As You Like It* [Act II, sc. 7]

HONEYSUCKLE

Woodbine

HERO

And bid her steal into the pleached bower.
Where HONEYSUCKLES, ripen'd by the sun,
Forbid the sun to enter.

—*Much Ado About Nothing* [Act III, sc. 1]

URSULA

So angle we for Beatrice; who even now
Is couched in the WOODBINE coverture.

—*Much Ado About Nothing* [Act III, sc. 1]

TITANIA

Sleep thou, and I will wind thee in my arms.
So doth the WOODBINE,
the sweet HONEYSUCKLE
Gently entwist; the female ivy so
Enrings the barky fingers of the elm.

—*A Midsummer Night's Dream* [Act IV, sc. 1]

HOSTESS / MISTRESS QUICKLY

O thou HONEYSUCKLE villain.

—*Henry IV, Pt. 2* [Act II, sc. 1]

OBERON

I know a bank where the wild thyme blows,
Where oxlips and the nodding violet grows,
Quite over-canopied
with luscious WOODBINE.

—*A Midsummer Night's Dream* [Act II, sc. 1]

HYSSOP

IAGO

'Tis in ourselves that we are thus or thus.
Our bodies are our gardens,
to the which our wills are gardeners;
so that if we will plant nettles or sow lettuce,
set HYSSOP, and weed up thyme,
supply it with one gender
of herbs or distract it with many,
either to have it sterile
with idleness, or maimed with industry,
why the power and corrigible authority
of this lies in our wills.

—*Othello* [Act I, sc. 3]

INSANE ROOT

BANQUO

Were such things here as we do speak about?
Or have we eaten on the INSANE ROOT
That takes the reason prisoner?

—*Macbeth* [Act I, sc. 3]

IVY

TITANIA

The female IVY so
Enrings the barky fingers of the elm.

—*A Midsummer Night's Dream* [Act IV, sc. 1]

PROSPERO

That now he was
The IVY which had hid my princely trunk
And suck'd my verdure out on't.

—*Tempest* [Act I, sc. 2]

ADRIANA

If aught possess thee from me,
it is dross,
Usurping IVY,
brier, or idle moss;
Who, all for want of pruning,
with intrusion
Infect thy sap and
live on thy confusion.

—*Comedy of Errors* [Act II, sc. 2]

SHEPHERD

They have scared away two of my best sheep,
which I fear the wolf will sooner find than the
master; if anywhere I have them 'tis by the
seaside browsing of IVY.

—*Winter's Tale* [Act III, sc. 3]

PIRITHOUS

His head's yellow,
Hard hair'd and curl'd,
thick twin'd like IVY tops,
Not to undo with thunder.

—*Two Noble Kinsmen* [Act IV, sc. 2]

KECKSIES

BURGUNDY

And nothing teems
But hateful docks, rough thistles,
KECKSIES, burs,
Losing both beauty and utility.

—*Henry V* [Act V, sc. 2]

KNOT-GRASS

LYSANDER

Get you gone, you dwarf;
You minimus, of hindering
KNOT-GRASS made;
You bead, you acorn.

—*A Midsummer Night's Dream* [Act III, sc. 2]

LADY-SMOCKS /
CUCKOO-FLOWERS

SONG OF SPRING

... LADY-SMOCKS all silver-white,
And cuckoo-buds of yellow hue,
Do paint the meadows with delight.

—*Love's Labour's Lost* [Act V, sc. 2]

CORDELIA

He was met even now
As mad as the vex'd sea; singing aloud;
crown'd with rank fumiter and furrow-weeds,
With burdocks, hemlock, nettles,
CUCKOO-FLOWERS,
In our sustaining corn.

—*King Lear* [Act IV, sc. 4]

LARK'S-HEELS

SONG [BOY]

Marigolds on deathbeds blowing,
LARK'S-HEELS trim;
All dear Nature's children sweet
Lie 'fore bride and bridegroom's feet.

—*Two Noble Kinsmen* [Act I, sc. 1]

LAVENDER

PERDITA

Here's flowers for you;
Hot LAVENDER, mints, savory, marjoram.

—Winter's Tale [Act IV, sc. 4]

LEEK

THISBE

His eyes were green as LEEKS.

—A Midsummer Night's Dream [Act V, sc. 1]

PISTOL

Tell him I'll knock his LEEK about his pate
upon Saint Davy's Day.

—Henry V [Act IV, sc. 1]

FLUELLEN

If your majesties is remembered of it, the
Welshmen did good service in a garden where
LEEKS did grow, wearing LEEKS in the
Monmouth caps; which your majesty knows to
this hour is an honourable badge of the service;
and I do believe your majesty takes no scorn to
wear the LEEK upon Saint Tavy's Day.

—Henry V [Act IV, sc. 7]

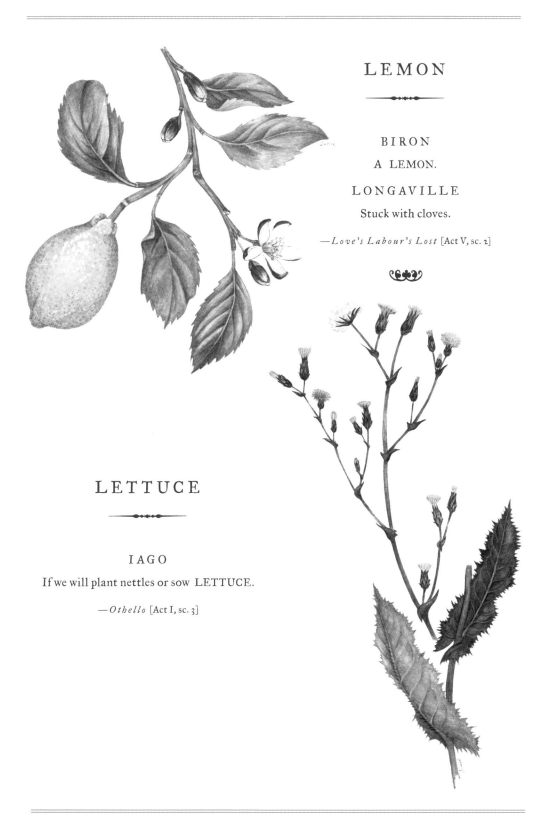

LEMON

BIRON

A LEMON.

LONGAVILLE

Stuck with cloves.

—*Love's Labour's Lost* [Act V, sc. 2]

LETTUCE

IAGO

If we will plant nettles or sow LETTUCE.

—*Othello* [Act I, sc. 3]

LILY / LILY OF THE VALLEY

PERDITA

LILIES of all kinds,
The flower-de-luce being one!

—*Winter's Tale* [Act IV, sc. 4]

LAUNCE

Look you, she is as white
as a LILY and as small as a wand.

—*Two Gentlemen of Verona* [Act II, sc. 3]

PRINCESS OF FRANCE

Now by my maiden honour, yet as pure
As the unsullied LILY.

—*Love's Labour's Lost* [Act V, sc. 2]

KATHERINE OF ARAGON

Like the LILY
That once was mistress of the field and flourish'd,
I'll hang my head, and perish.

—*Henry VIII* [Act III, sc. 1]

JULIA

The air hath starved the roses in her cheeks,
And pinch'd the LILY-tincture
of her face.

—*Two Gentlemen of Verona* [Act IV, sc. 4]

FLUTE / THISBE

Most radiant Pyramus,
most LILY-WHITE of hue.

—*A Midsummer Night's Dream* [Act III, sc. 1]

For sweetest things turn sourest by their deeds;
LILIES that fester smell far worse than weeds.

—*Sonnet XCIV*

FLUTE / THISBE

These LILY lips.

—*A Midsummer Night's Dream* [Act V, sc. 1]

CRANMER

Yet a virgin,
A most unspotted LILY shall she pass
To the ground.

—*Henry VIII* [Act V, sc. 5]

IACHIMO

How bravely thou becomes thy bed,
fresh LILY!

—*Cymbeline* [Act II, sc. 2]

MARCUS

O, had the monster seen those LILY hands
Tremble, like aspen leaves, upon a lute.

—*Titus Andronicus* [Act II, sc. 4]

TROILUS

Give me swift transportance to those fields,
Where I may wallow in the LILY beds ...

—*Troilus and Cressida* [Act III, sc. 2]

TITUS

Fresh tears
Stood upon her cheeks, as doth the honey-dew
Upon a gather'd LILY almost wither'd.

—*Titus Andronicus* [Act III, sc. 1]

CONSTANCE

Of Nature's gifts thou may'st
with LILIES boast,
And with the half-blown rose.

—*King John* [Act III, sc. 1]

GUIDERIUS

O sweetest, fairest LILY!
My brother wears thee not the one half so well,
As when thou grew'st thyself.

—*Cymbeline* [Act IV, sc. 2]

SALISBURY

To gild refined gold, to paint the LILY,
To throw a perfume on the violet,
... Is wasteful and ridiculous excess.

—*King John* [Act IV, sc. 2]

KENT

A LILY-LIVERED, action taking knave.

—*King Lear* [Act II, sc. 2]

MACBETH

Thou LILY-LIVER'D boy.

—*Macbeth* [Act V, sc. 3]

Nor did I wonder at the LILY'S white,
Nor praise the deep vermilion of the rose.

—*Sonnet XCVIII*

The LILY I condemned for thy hand.

—*Sonnet XCIX*

Their silent war of LILIES and of roses
Which Tarquin view'd in her fair face's field.

—*Lucrece*

Her LILY hand her rosy cheek lies under,
Cozening the pillow of a lawful kiss.

—*Lucrece*

The colour in thy face
That even for anger makes the LILY pale,
And the red rose blush at her own disgrace.

—*Lucrece*

A LILY pale with damask die to grace her.

—*Passionate Pilgrim*

Full gently now she takes him by the hand,
A LILY prison'd in a jail of snow.

—*Venus and Adonis*

She locks her LILY fingers one in one.

—*Venus and Adonis*

Whose wonted LILY white
With purple tears, that his wound wept,
was drench'd.

—*Venus and Adonis*

LINE TREE / LINDEN

ARIEL

All prisoners, sir,
In the LINE-GROVE which
weather-fends your cell.

-Tempest [Act V, sc. 1]

PROSPERO

Come, hang them on this LINE.

—Tempest [Act IV, sc. 1]

STEPHANO

Mistress LINE, is not this my jerkin?

—Tempest [Act IV, sc. 1]

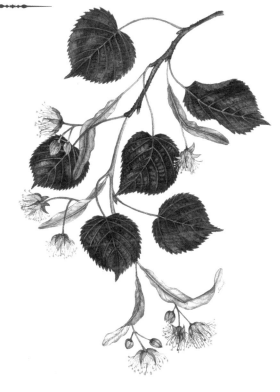

LOCUST

Carob Tree

IAGO

The food that to him now is as luscious
as LOCUSTS, shall
be to him shortly as bitter as coloquintida.

—Othello [Act I, sc. 3]

LONG PURPLES

Dead-Men's Fingers

GERTRUDE

There with fantastic garlands did she come
Of crow-flowers, nettles, daisies,
and LONG PURPLES,
That liberal shepherds give a grosser name,
But our cold maids do DEAD MEN'S
FINGERS call.

—*Hamlet* [Act IV, sc. 7]

MALLOW

ANTONIO

He'd sow it with nettle seed.

SEBASTIAN

Or docks, or MALLOWS.

—*Tempest* [Act II, sc. 1]

MANDRAKE / MANDRAGORA

CLEOPATRA

Give me to drink MANDRAGORA.

CHARMIAN

Why, madam?

CLEOPATRA

That I might sleep out this great gap of time
My Antony is away.

—*Antony and Cleopatra* [Act I, sc. 5]

IAGO

Not Poppy, nor MANDRAGORA,
Nor all the drowsy syrups in the world
Shall ever medicine thee to that sweet sleep
Which thou owdest yesterday.

—*Othello* [Act III, sc. 3]

JULIET

And shrieks like MANDRAKES'
torn out of the earth
That living mortals, hearing them, run mad.

—*Romeo and Juliet* [Act IV, sc. 3]

FALSTAFF

Thou whoreson MANDRAKE,
thou art fitter to be worn
in my cap than to wait at my heels.

—*Henry IV, Pt. 2* [Act I, sc. 2]

FALSTAFF

...the very genius of famine; yet lecherous
as a monkey, and the whores called him
MANDRAKE: a' came ever in the rearward of the
fashion, and sung those tunes to the overscutched
huswives that he heard the carmen whistle, and
swear they were his fancies or his good-nights.

—*Henry IV, Pt. 2* [Act III, sc. 2]

SUFFOLK

Would curses kill,
as doth the MANDRAKE'S groan.

—*Henry VI, Pt. 2* [Act III, sc. 2]

MARIGOLD / MARY-BUD

PERDITA

The MARIGOLD that goes to bed wi' the sun,
And with him rises weeping; these are flowers
Of middle summer.

—*Winter's Tale* [Act IV, sc. 4]

MARINA

The purple violets and MARIGOLDS
Shall, as a carpet, hang upon thy grave
While summer-days do last.

—*Pericles* [Act IV, sc. 1]

SONG [CLOTEN]

And winking MARY-BUDS begin
To ope their golden eyes.

—*Cymbeline* [Act II, sc. 3]

SONG [BOY]

MARIGOLDS on death-beds blowing.

—*Two Noble Kinsmen* [Act I, sc. 1]

Great princes' favourites their fair leaves spread
But as the MARIGOLDS at the sun's eye
And in themselves their pride lies buried,
For at a frown they in their glory die.

—*Sonnet XXV*

Her eyes, like MARIGOLDS,
had sheathed their light,
And canopied in darkness sweetly lay,
Till they might open to adorn the day.

—*Lucrece*

MARJORAM

PERDITA

Here's flowers for you;
Hot lavender, mints, savory, MARJORAM.

—*Winter's Tale* [Act IV, sc. 4]

LAVATCH / CLOWN

Indeed, sir, she was the
SWEET MARJORAM of the
Salad, or rather the Herb-of-grace.

—*All's Well That Ends Well* [Act IV, sc. 5]

The lily I condemned for thy hand,
And buds of MARJORAM had stol'n thy hair.

—*Sonnet XCIX*

LEAR
Give the word.

EDGAR
SWEET MARJORAM.

LEAR
Pass.

—*King Lear* [Act IV, sc. 6]

MEDLAR

TOUCHSTONE

Truly the tree yields bad fruit.

ROSALIND

I'll graff it with you, and then I shall
graff it with a MEDLAR;
then it will be the earliest fruit in the country,
for you'll be rotten ere you be
half ripe, and that's the right virtue
of the MEDLAR.

—*As You Like It* [Act IV, sc. 3]

MERCUTIO

If love be blind, love cannot hit the mark.
Now will he sit under a MEDLAR tree
And wish his mistress were that kind of fruit
As maids call MEDLARS
when they laugh alone.
Romeo, that she were O, that she were
An open arse, thou a poperin' pear!

—*Romeo and Juliet* [Act II, sc. 1]

APEMANTUS

There's a MEDLAR for thee, eat it.

TIMON

On what I hate I feed not.

APEMANTUS

Dost hate a MEDLAR?

TIMON

Ay, though it looks like thee.

APEMANTUS

An thou hadst hated meddlers sooner, thou
Shouldst have loved thyself better now.

—*Timon of Athens* [Act IV, sc. 3]

LUCIO

They would have married me to the rotten
MEDLAR.

—*Measure for Measure* [Act IV, sc. 3]

MINT

PERDITA

Here's flowers for you;
Hot lavender, MINTS, savory, marjoram.

—*Winter's Tale* [Act IV, sc. 4]

ARMANDO

I am that flower,

DUMAIN

That MINT.

LONGAVILLE

That columbine.

—*Love's Labour's Lost* [Act V, sc. 2]

MISTLETOE

TAMORA

The trees, though summer,
yet forlorn and lean,
O'ercome with moss
and baleful MISTLETOE.

—*Titus Andronicus* [Act II, sc. 3]

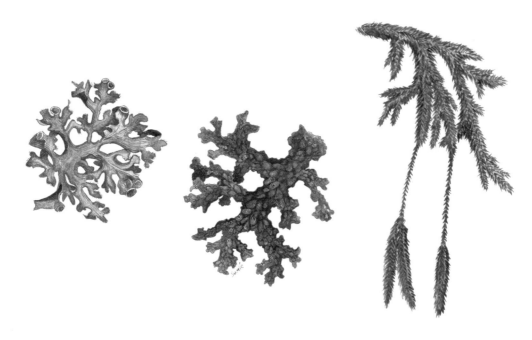

MOSS

ADRIANA

If ought possess thee from me, it is dross,
Usurping ivy, brier, or idle MOSS.

—Comedy of Errors [Act II, sc. 2]

TAMORA

The trees, though summer,
yet forlorn and lean,
O'ercome with MOSS and baleful mistletoe.

—Titus Andronicus [Act II, sc. 3]

APEMANTUS

These MOSS'D trees,
That have outlived the eagle.

—Timon of Athens [Act IV, sc. 2]

HOTSPUR

Steeples and MOSS-GROWN towers.

—Henry IV, Pt. 1 [Act III, sc. 1]

OLIVER

Under an oak whose boughs
were MOSSED with age,
And high top bald with dry antiquity.

—As You Like It [Act IV, sc. 3]

ARVIRAGUS

...and furr'd MOSS besides,
when flowers are none,
To winter-ground thy corse.

—Cymbeline [Act IV, sc. 2]

MULBERRIES

TITANIA

Feed him with apricocks and dewberries,
With purple grapes, green figs,
and MULBERRIES.

—*A Midsummer Night's Dream* [Act III, sc. 1]

The birds such pleasure took,
That some would sing, some other in their bills
Would bring him MULBERRIES
and ripe-red cherries;
He fed them with his sight,
they him with BERRIES.

—*Venus and Adonis*

VOLUMNIA

Thy stout heart,
Now humble as the ripest MULBERRY
That will not bear the handling.

—*Coriolanus* [Act III, sc. 2]

PROLOGUE / QUINCE

Thisbe tarrying in MULBERRY shade.

—*A Midsummer Night's Dream* [Act V, sc. 1]

WOOER

Palamon is gone
Is gone to the wood to gather MULBERRIES.

—*Two Noble Kinsmen* [Act IV, sc. 1]

MUSHROOM / TOADSTOOL

PROSPERO

You demi-puppets, that
By moonshine do the
GREENSOUR RINGLETS make,
Whereof the ewe not bites, and you whose pastime
Is to make midnight MUSHRUMPS.

—*Tempest* [Act V, sc. 1]

FAIRY

And I serve the Fairy Queen,
To dew her ORBS UPON THE GREEN.

—*A Midsummer Night's Dream* [Act II, sc. 1]

AJAX

TOADSTOOL, learn me the proclamation.

—*Troilus and Cressida* [Act II, sc. 1]

MISTRESS QUICKLY

And nightly, meadow-fairies, look you sing,
Like to the Garter's compass, IN A RING;
The expressure that it bears, green let it be,
More fertile-fresh than all the field to see.

—*Merry Wives of Windsor* [Act V, sc. 5]

TITANIA

To dance OUR RINGLETS
to the whistling wind

—*A Midsummer Night's Dream* [Act II, sc. 1]

MUSTARD

FALSTAFF

Hang him, baboon! His wit's as thick as
Tewksbury MUSTARD; there is no more
conceit in him than a mallet.

—*Henry IV, Pt. 2* [Act II, sc. 4]

GRUMIO

What say you to a piece of beef and MUSTARD?

KATHARINE

A dish that I do love to feed upon.

GRUMIO

Ay, but the MUSTARD
is too hot a little.

KATHARINE

Why then, the beef,
and let the MUSTARD rest.

GRUMIO

Nay, then, I will not;
you shall have the MUSTARD,
Or else you get no beef of Grumio.

KATHARINE

Then both, or one, or anything thou wilt.

GRUMIO

Why then, the MUSTARD without the beef.

—*Taming of the Shrew* [Act IV, sc. 3]

BOTTOM

Where's the Mounsieur MUSTARDSEED?

MUSTARDSEED

Ready.

BOTTOM

Give me your neaf, Mounsieur
MUSTARDSEED. Pray you,
leave your courtesy, good Mounsieur.

MUSTARDSEED

What's your will?

BOTTOM

Nothing, good Mounsieur, but to help
Cavalery Cobweb to scratch.

—*A Midsummer Night's Dream* [Act IV, sc. 1]

ROSALIND

Where learned you that oath, fool?

TOUCHSTONE

Of a certain knight that swore by his honour
they were good pancakes,
and swore by his honour
the MUSTARD was naught;
now I'll stand to it,
the pancakes were naught,
and the MUSTARD was good,
yet the knight not forsworn . . .
you are not forsworn; no more
was this knight swearing by his honour,
for he never had any; or if he had,
he had sworn it away before he ever saw
those cakes or that MUSTARD.

—*As You Like It* [Act I, sc. 2]

TITANIA

Pease-blossom! Cobweb! Moth! and
MUSTARDSEED! . . .

BOTTOM

Good Master MUSTARDSEED,
I know your patience well;
the same cowardly giant-like ox-beef hath
devoured many a gentleman
of your house: I promise you your kindred
hath made my eyes water ere now.
I desire your more acquaintance,
good Master MUSTARDSEED.

—*A Midsummer Night's Dream* [Act III, sc. 1]

MYRTLE

EUPHRONIUS

I was of late as petty to his ends
As did the morn-dew on the MYRTLE-LEAF
To his grand sea.

—*Antony and Cleopatra* [Act III, sc. 10]

Venus, with young Adonis sitting by her,
Under a MYRTLE shade began to woo him.

—*Passionate Pilgrim*

ISABELLA

Merciful Heaven,
Thou rather with thy sharp and sulphurous bolt
Split'st the unwedgeable and gnarled oak
Than the soft MYRTLE.

—*Measure for Measure* [Act II, sc. 2]

Then sad she hasteth to a MYRTLE grove.

—*Venus and Adonis*

NETTLES

CORDELIA

Crown'd with rank fumiter and furrow-weeds,
With burdocks, hemlock, NETTLES,
cuckoo-flowers.

—King Lear [Act IV, sc. 4]

GERTRUDE

Crow-flowers, NETTLES, daisies,
and long purples.

—Hamlet [Act IV, sc. 7]

ANTONIO

He'd sow't with NETTLE-SEED.

—Tempest [Act II, sc. 1]

SATURNINUS

Look for thy reward
Among the NETTLES at the elder tree.

—Titus Andronicus [Act II, sc. 3]

RICHARD II

Yield STINGING NETTLES to my enemies.

—Richard II [Act III, sc. 2]

HOTSPUR

I tell you, my lord fool, out of this NETTLE,
danger,
we pluck this flower, safety.

—Henry IV, Pt. 1 [Act II, sc. 3]

ELY

The strawberry grows underneath
the NETTLE.

—Henry V [Act I, sc. 1]

CRESSIDA

I'll spring up in his tears, an 'twere a NETTLE
against May.

—Troilus and Cressida [Act I, sc. 2]

LEONTES

Sully the purity and whiteness of my sheets?
Which to preserve is sleep; which being spotted
Is goads, thorns, NETTLES, tails of wasps.

—Winter's Tale [Act I, sc. 2]

MENENIUS

We call a NETTLE but a NETTLE, and
the fault of fools but folly.

—Coriolanus [Act II, sc. 1]

PALAMON

Who do bear thy yoke
As 'twere a wreath of roses, yet is heavier
Than lead itself, stings more than NETTLES.

—*Two Noble Kinsmen* [Act V, sc. 1]

IAGO

If we will plant NETTLES or sow lettuce.

—*Othello* [Act I, sc. 3]

NUTMEG / MACE

ORLEANS

He's of the colour of the NUTMEG.

—Henry V [Act III, sc. 7]

SHEPHERD'S SON / CLOWN

I must have saffron to colour the warden
pies; MACE; dates?—none, that's out of my note;
NUTMEGS, seven; a race or two of ginger,
but that I may beg;
four pound of prunes, and as many of
raisins o' the sun.

—Winter's Tale [Act IV, sc. 3]

ARMANDO

The omnipotent Mars, of lances the almighty,
Gave Hector a gift—

DUMAIN

A gilt NUTMEG.

—Love's Labour's Lost [Act V, sc. 2]

OAK

PROSPERO

To the dread rattling thunder
Have I given fire,
and rifted JOVE'S STOUT OAK
With his own bolt.

—Tempest [Act V, sc. 1]

WARWICK

Whose top-branch overpeer'd JOVE'S
SPREADING TREE
And kept low shrubs from winter's powerful
wind.

—Henry VI, Pt. 3 [Act V, sc. 2]

BENEDICK

An OAK with but one
green leaf on it would
have answered her.

—Much Ado About Nothing [Act II, sc. 1]

ISABELLA

Thou split'st the unwedgable and gnarled OAK.

—Measure for Measure [Act II, sc. 2]

FIRST LORD

He lay along
Under an OAK, whose antique root peeps out
Upon the brook that brawls along this wood.

—As You Like It [Act II, sc. 1]

OLIVER

Under an OAK,
whose boughs were mossed with age,
And high top bald with dry antiquity.

—As You Like It [Act IV, sc. 3]

MARCIUS

He that depends
Upon your favours swims with fins of lead
And hews down OAKS with rushes.

—Coriolanus [Act I, sc. 1]

FENTON

Tonight at HERNE'S OAK,
just 'twixt twelve and one.

—Merry Wives of Windsor [Act IV, sc. 6]

ROSALIND

It may well be called JOVE'S TREE,
when it drops
forth such fruit.

—As You Like It [Act III, sc. 2]

FALSTAFF

Be you in the park about midnight at
HERNE'S OAK, and you shall see wonders.

—Merry Wives of Windsor [Act V, sc. 1]

PETER QUINCE

At the DUKE'S OAK we meet.

—A Midsummer Night's Dream [Act I, sc. 2]

MISTRESS PAGE

They are all couched in a pit hard by
HERNE'S OAK....

MISTRESS FORD

The hour draws on. To the OAK, to the OAK!

—Merry Wives of Windsor [Act V, sc. 3]

MISTRESS QUICKLY

Till 'tis one o'clock
Our dance of custom round about the OAK.

—*Merry Wives of Windsor* [Act V, sc. 5]

TIMON

The OAKS bear mast, the briers scarlet hips.

—*Timon of Athens* [Act IV, sc. 3]

NESTOR

When the splitting wind
Makes flexible the knees of knotted OAKS.

—*Troilus and Cressida* [Act I, sc. 3]

VOLUMNIA

He comes the third time home with
the OAKEN garland.

—*Coriolanus* [Act II, sc. 1]

TIMON

That numberless upon me struck as leaves
Do on the OAK, have with one winter's brush
Fell from their boughs, and left me open, bare
For every storm that blows.

—*Timon of Athens* [Act IV, sc. 3]

IAGO

She that so young could give out such a seeming
To seal her father's eyes up close as OAK.

—*Othello* [Act III, sc. 3]

PROSPERO

If thou more murmur'st, I will rend an OAK,
And peg thee in his knotty entrails.

—*Tempest* [Act I, sc. 2]

ARVIRAGUS

To thee the reed is as the OAK.

—*Cymbeline* [Act IV, sc. 2]

KING LEAR

OAK-cleaving thunderbolts.

—*King Lear* [Act III, sc. 2]

NATHANIEL

Though to myself forsworn,
to thee I'll faithful prove;
Those thoughts to me were OAKS,
to thee like osiers bow'd.

—*Love's Labour's Lost* [Act IV, sc. 2]

VOLUMNIA

To a cruel war I sent him,
from whence he returned,
his brows bound with OAK.

—*Coriolanus* [Act I, sc. 3]

MESSENGER

And many strokes, though with a little axe,
Hew down and fell the hardest-timber'd OAK.

—*Henry VI, Pt. 3* [Act II, sc. 1]

MISTRESS PAGE

There is an old tale goes that Herne the Hunter,
Sometime a keeper here in Windsor Forest,
Doth all the winter time at still midnight
Walk round about an OAK,
with great ragg'd horns ...

MASTER PAGE

Why yet there want not many that do fear
In deep of night to walk by
this HERNE'S OAK ...

MISTRESS FORD

That Falstaff at that OAK shall meet with us.

—*Merry Wives of Windsor* [Act IV, sc. 4]

MONTANO

What ribs of OAK,
when mountains melt on them,
Can hold the mortise?

—*Othello* [Act II, sc. 1]

COMINIUS

He proved best man i' the field, and for his meed
Was brow-bound with the OAK.

—*Coriolanus* [Act II, sc. 2]

SECOND SENATOR

The worthy fellow is our general; he's the rock,
the OAK, not to be wind-shaken.

—*Coriolanus* [Act V, sc. 2]

VOLUMNIA

To charge thy sulphur with a bolt
That should but rive an OAK.

—*Coriolanus* [Act V, sc. 3]

CASCA

I have seen tempests when the scolding winds
Have rived the knotty OAKS.

—*Julius Cæsar* [Act I, sc. 3]

MESSENGER

About his head he wears the winner's OKE.

—*Two Noble Kinsmen* [Act IV, sc. 2]

Time's glory is ...
To dry the old OAK'S sap.

—*Lucrece*

PAULINA

As ever OAK or stone was sound.

—*Winter's Tale* [Act II, sc. 3]

OATS

IRIS

Ceres, most bounteous lady, thy rich leas
Of wheat, rye, barley, vetches,
OATS, and pease.

—Tempest [Act IV, sc. 1]

SONG OF SPRING

When shepherds pipe on OATEN straws.

—Love's Labour's Lost [Act V, sc. 2]

BOTTOM

Truly a peck of provender;
I could munch your good dry OATS.

—A Midsummer Night's Dream [Act IV, sc. 1]

GRUMIO

Ay, sir, they be ready;
the OATS have eaten the horses.

—Taming of the Shrew [Act III, sc. 2]

FIRST CARRIER

Poor fellow, never joyed since the price of
OATS rose—it was the death of him.

—Henry IV, Pt. 1 [Act II, sc. 1]

CAPTAIN

I cannot draw a cart, not eat dried OATS,
If it be a man's work, I'll do it.

—King Lear [Act V, sc. 3]

JAILER'S DAUGHTER

Some two hundred bottles,
And twenty strike of OATS,
but he'll ne'er have her.

—Two Noble Kinsmen [Act V, sc. 2]

OLIVE

CLARENCE

To whom the heavens in thy nativity
Adjudged an OLIVE branch.

—*Henry VI, Pt.* 3 [Act IV, sc. 6]

ALCIBIADES

Bring me into your city,
And I will use the OLIVE
with my sword.

—*Timon of Athens* [Act V, sc. 4]

CÆSAR

Prove this a prosperous day,
the three-nook'd world
Shall bear the OLIVE freely.

—*Antony and Cleopatra* [Act IV, sc. 6]

ROSALIND

If you will know my house
'Tis at the tuft of OLIVES
here hard by.

—*As You Like It* [Act III, sc. 5]

OLIVER

Where, in the purlieus of this forest stands
A sheepcote fenced about with OLIVE trees?

—*As You Like It* [Act IV, sc. 3]

VIOLA

I bring no overture of war,
no taxation of homage;
I hold the OLIVE in my hand;
my words are as full of peace
as matter.

—*Twelfth Night* [Act I, sc. 5]

WESTMORELAND

Peace puts forth her OLIVE everywhere.

—*Henry IV, Pt.* 2 [Act IV, sc. 4]

And peace proclaims OLIVES of endless age.

—*Sonnet CVII*

ONION

BOTTOM

And, most dear Actors, eat no ONIONS
nor garlic, for we are to utter sweet breath.

—A Midsummer Night's Dream [Act IV, sc. 2]

LAFEU

Mine eyes smell ONIONS,
I shall weep anon:
Good Tom Drum, lend me a handkercher.

—All's Well That Ends Well [Act V, sc. 3]

ENOBARBUS

Indeed the tears
live in an ONION that should
water this sorrow.

—Antony and Cleopatra [Act I, sc. 2]

ENOBARBUS

Look, they weep,
And I, an ass, am ONION-eyed.

—Antony and Cleopatra [Act IV, sc. 2]

LORD

And if the boy have not a woman's gift
To rain a shower of commanded tears,
An ONION will do well for such a shift,
Which in a napkin being close conveyed
Shall in despite enforce a watery eye.

—Taming of the Shrew [Induction, sc. 1]

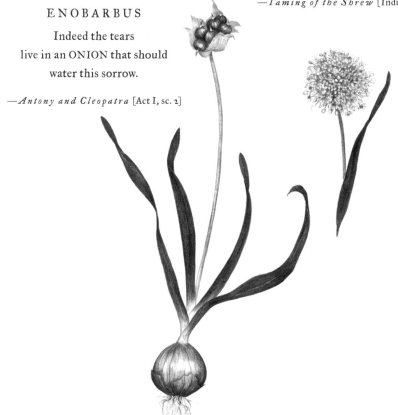

ORANGE

BEATRICE

The count is neither sad nor sick, nor merry
nor well; but civil count, civil as an ORANGE,
and something of that jealous complexion.

—*Much Ado About Nothing* [Act II, sc. 1]

MENENIUS

You wear out a good wholesome fornoon
in hearing a cause between
an ORANGE-wife and a fosset-seller.

—*Coriolanus* [Act II, sc. 1]

CLAUDIO

Give not this rotten ORANGE to your friend.

—*Much Ado About Nothing* [Act IV, sc. 1]

OXLIP

PERDITA

Bold OXLIPS,
The crown imperial.

—*Winter's Tale* [Act IV, sc. 4]

OBERON

I know a bank where the wild thyme blows,
Where OXLIPS and
the nodding violet grows.

—*A Midsummer Night's Dream* [Act II, sc. 1]

SONG [BOY]

OXLIPS in their cradles growing.

—*Two Noble Kinsmen* [Act I, sc. 1]

PALM

ROSALIND

Look here what I found on a PALM tree.

—As You Like It [Act III, sc. 2]

HAMLET

As love between them like the PALM
might flourish.

—Hamlet [Act V, sc. 2]

VOLUMNIA

And bear the PALM
for having bravely shed
Thy wife and children's blood.

—Coriolanus [Act V, sc. 3]

CASSIUS

And bear the PALM alone.

—Julius Cæsar [Act I, sc. 2]

PAINTER

You shall see him a PALM
in Athens again,
and flourish with the highest.

—Timon of Athens [Act V, sc. 1]

THE VISION

Enter, solemnly tripping one after another, six
personages, clad in white robes,
wearing on their heads garlands of bays
and golden vizards on their faces,
branches of bays or PALM in their hands.

—Henry VIII [Act IV, sc. 2]

PANSY

*Love-in-idleness*Cupid's Flower*

OPHELIA

There is PANSIES—that's for thoughts.

—*Hamlet* [Act IV, sc. 5]

LUCENTIO

But see, while idly I stood looking on,
I found the effect of LOVE-IN-IDLENESS.

—*Taming of the Shrew* [Act I, sc. 1]

OBERON

Yet mark'd I where the bolt of Cupid fell:
It fell upon a little western flower,
Before milk-white, now purple with Love's wound,
And maidens call it LOVE-IN-IDLENESS.
Fetch me that flower; the herb I show'd thee once;
The juice of it on sleeping eyelids laid
Will make or man or woman madly dote
Upon the next live creature that it sees.

—*A Midsummer Night's Dream* [Act II, sc. 1]

OBERON

Dian's bud o'er CUPID'S FLOWER
Hath such free and blessed power.

—*A Midsummer Night's Dream* [Act IV, sc. 1]

PARMACETI

Shepherd's Purse

HOTSPUR

I then, all smarting with my wounds being cold,
To be so pester'd with a popinjay,
Out of my grief and my impatience,
Answer'd neglectingly I know not what,
He should or he should not; for he made me mad
To see him shine so brisk and smell so sweet
And talk so like a waiting-gentlewoman
Of guns and drums and wounds,—God save the mark!—
And telling me the sovereign'st thing on earth
Was PARMACETI for an inward bruise;
And that it was great pity, so it was,
This villanous salt-petre should be digg'd
Out of the bowels of the harmless earth,
Which many a good tall fellow had destroy'd . . .

—Henry IV, Pt. I [Act I, sc. 3]

PARSLEY

BIONDELLO

I knew a wench married in an afternoon
as she went to the garden
for PARSLEY to stuff a rabbit.

—Taming of the Shrew [Act IV, sc. 4]

PEACH

POMPEY

There is here one Master Caper, at the suit
of Master Three-pile the mercer, for some
four suits of PEACH-coloured satin,
which now peaches him a beggar.

—*Measure for Measure* [Act IV, sc. 3]

PRINCE HENRY

Take note how many pair of
silk stockings thou hast,
viz., these, and those
that were thy
PEACH-coloured ones!

—*Henry IV, Pt. 2* [Act II, sc. 2]

PEAR

Warden *Popering*

FALSTAFF

I warrant they would whip me with their fine
wits till I were as crest-fallen as a dried PEAR.

—*Merry Wives of Windsor* [Act IV, sc. 5]

PAROLLES

Your virginity, your old virginity, is like one of
our French withered PEARS, it looks ill, it eats
drily; marry, 'tis a withered PEAR; it was for-
merly better; marry, yet 'tis a withered PEAR.

—*All's Well That Ends Well* [Act I, sc. 1]

SHEPHERD'S SON / CLOWN

I must have saffron
to colour the WARDEN pies.

—*Winter's Tale* [Act IV, sc. 3]

MERCUTIO

Romeo, that she were O, that she were
An open arse, thou a Poperin' PEAR.

—*Romeo and Juliet* [Act II, sc. 1]

PEAS

*Peascod*Peaseblossom*Squash*

IRIS

Ceres, most bounteous lady, thy rich leas
Of wheat, rye, barley, vetches, oats, and PEASE.

—*Tempest* [Act IV, sc. 1]

SECOND CARRIER

PEAS and beans are as dank here as a dog.

—*Henry IV, Pt. 1* [Act II, sc. 1]

BIRON

This fellow picks up wit as pigeons PEASE.

—*Love's Labour's Lost* [Act V, sc. 2]

BOTTOM

I had rather have a handful or two
of dried PEAS.

—*A Midsummer Night's Dream* [Act IV, sc. 1]

FOOL

That's a shelled PEASCOD.

—*King Lear* [Act I, sc. 4]

TOUCHSTONE

I remember the wooing of a PEASCOD
instead of her.

—*As You Like It* [Act II, sc. 4]

MALVOLIO

Not yet old enough to be a man,
nor young enough for a boy;
as a SQUASH is before 'tis a PEASCOD,
or a codling when 'tis almost an apple.

—*Twelfth Night* [Act I, sc. 5]

HOSTESS / MISTRESS QUICKLY

I have known thee these twenty-nine years
come PEASCOD-time.

—*Henry IV, Pt. 2* [Act II, sc. 4]

LEONTES

How like, methought,
I then was to this kernel,
This SQUASH, this gentleman.

—*Winter's Tale* [Act I, sc. 2]

BOTTOM

I pray you, commend me to Mistress
SQUASH, your mother, and to Master
PEASCOD, your father.

—*A Midsummer Night's Dream* [Act III, sc. 1]

PEPPER

HOTSPUR

Such protest of
PEPPER-gingerbread.

—*Henry IV, Pt.* 1 [Act III, sc. 1]

POINS

Pray God,
you have not murdered
some of them.

FALSTAFF

Nay, that's past praying for,
for I have PEPPERED
two of them.

—*Henry IV, Pt.* 1 [Act II, sc. 4]

FALSTAFF

And I have not forgotten what
the inside of a church is made of,
I am a PEPPER-CORN, a brewer's horse.

—*Henry IV, Pt.* 1 [Act III, sc. 3]

FALSTAFF

I have led my ragamuffins,
where they are PEPPERED.

—*Henry IV, Pt.* 1 [Act V, sc. 3]

FORD

He cannot 'scape me, 'tis impossible he
should; he cannot creep into
a halfpenny purse or into a PEPPER-BOX.

—*Merry Wives of Windsor* [Act III, sc. 5]

MERCUTIO

I am PEPPERED, I warrant, for this world.

—*Romeo and Juliet* [Act III, sc. 1]

SIR ANDREW AGUECHEEK

Here's the challenge, read it;
I warrant there's vinegar and PEPPER in't.

—*Twelfth Night* [Act III, sc. 4]

PIG-NUT

CALIBAN

I prythee let me bring thee where crabs grow;
And I with my long nails
will dig thee PIG-NUTS.

—*Tempest* [Act II, sc. 2]

PINE

PROSPERO

She did confine thee,
By help of her more potent ministers
And in her most unmitigable rage,
Into a cloven PINE . . .

—*Tempest* [Act I, sc. 2]

PROSPERO

It was mine art,
When I arrived and heard thee,
that made gape
The PINE and let thee out.

—*Tempest* [Act I, sc. 2]

SUFFOLK

Thus droops this lofty PINE
and hangs his sprays.

—*Henry VI, Pt. 2* [Act II, sc. 3]

PROSPERO

And by the spurs plucked up
The PINE and cedar.

—*Tempest* [Act V, sc. 1]

AGAMEMNON

As knots, by the conflux of meeting sap,
Infect the sound PINE and divert his grain
Tortive and errant from his course of growth.

—*Troilus and Cressida* [Act I, sc. 3]

ANTONY

Where yonder PINE does stand
I shall discover all.

—*Antony and Cleopatra* [Act IV, sc. 12]

ANTONY

This PINE is bark'd
That overtopped them all.

—*Antony and Cleopatra* [Act IV, sc. 12]

BELARIUS

As the rudest wind
That by the top doth take the mountain PINE,
And make him stoop to the vale.

—*Cymbeline* [Act IV, sc. 2]

FIRST LORD

Behind the tuft of PINES I met them.

—*Winter's Tale* [Act II, sc. 1]

RICHARD II

But when from under this terrestrial ball
He fires the proud top of the eastern PINES.

—*Richard II* [Act III, sc. 2]

ANTONIO

You may as well forbid the mountain PINES
To wag their high tops and to make no noise,
When they are fretten with the gusts of heaven.

—*Merchant of Venice* [Act IV, sc. 1]

Ay me! the bark peel'd from the lofty PINE,
His leaves will wither, and his sap decay;
So must my soul, her bark being peel'd away.

—*Lucrece*

PLANE TREE

JAILER'S DAUGHTER

I have sent him where a cedar,
Higher than all the rest, spreads like a PLANE
Fast by a brook.

—*Two Noble Kinsmen* [Act II, sc. 6]

PLANTAIN

COSTARD

O sir, PLANTAIN, a plain PLANTAIN!
No l'envoy, no l'envoy; no salve, sir,
but a PLANTAIN.

—*Love's Labour's Lost* [Act III, sc. 1]

MOTH

By saying that a costard
was broken in a shin.
Then call'd you for the l'envoy?

COSTARD

True, and I for a
PLANTAIN.

—*Love's Labour's Lost*
[Act III, sc. 1]

ROMEO

Your PLANTAN-leafe is excellent for that.

BENVOLIO

For what, I pray thee?

ROMEO

For your broken shin.

—*Romeo and Juliet* [Act I, sc. 2]

PALAMON

These poor slight sores
Need not a PLANTAIN.

—*Two Noble Kinsmen*
[Act I, sc. 2]

PLUM

*Damsons*Prunes*

FALSTAFF

There's no more faith in thee
than in a stewed PRUNE.

—Henry IV, Pt. 1 [Act III, sc. 3]

HAMLET

The satirical rogue says here that old men
have grey beards, that their faces are wrinkled,
their eyes purging thick amber
and PLUM-tree gum.

—Hamlet [Act II, sc. 2]

SHEPHERD'S SON / CLOWN

Four pounds of PRUNES,
and as many of raisins o' the sun.

—Winter's Tale [Act IV, sc. 3]

SCHOOLMASTER

Have my rudiments been labored so long
with you, milked unto you, and, by a figure,
even the very PLUM broth and marrow of my
understanding laid upon you?

—Two Noble Kinsmen [Act III, sc. 5]

SIR HUGH EVANS

I will dance and eat PLUMS at your wedding.

—Merry Wives of Windsor [Act V, sc. 5]

SIMPCOX

A fall off a tree.

WIFE

A PLUM-TREE, master.

—Henry VI, Pt. 2 [Act II, sc. 1]

The mellow PLUM doth fall,
the green sticks fast,
Or, being early pluck'd, is sour to taste.

—Venus and Adonis

SLENDER

Three veneys for a dish of stewed PRUNES.

—Merry Wives of Windsor [Act I, sc. 1]

DOLL TEARSHEET

Hang him, rogue; he lives upon
mouldy stewed PRUNES and dried cakes.

—Henry IV, Pt. 2 [Act II, sc. 4]

CONSTANCE

Give it a PLUM, a cherry, and a fig.

—King John [Act II, sc. 1]

POMPEY

Longing—saving your honour's reverence—
for stewed PRUNES.

—Measure for Measure [Act II, sc. 1]

SECOND COUNTRYMAN

Hang him, PLUM porridge!
He wrestle? He roast eggs!

—Two Noble Kinsmen [Act II, sc. 3]

GLOUCESTER

Mass, thou lovedst PLUMS well
that wouldst venture so.

SIMPCOX

Alas, good master,
my wife desired some DAMSONS,
And made me climb with danger of my life.

—Henry VI, Pt. 2 [Act II, sc. 1]

POMPEY

And longing, as I said, for PRUNES.

—Measure for Measure [Act II, sc. 1]

POMPEY

You being then, if you be remembered,
cracking the stones of the foresaid PRUNES.

—Measure for Measure [Act II, sc. 1]

POMEGRANATE

LAFEU

You were beaten in Italy for picking a kernel
out of a POMEGRANATE.

—All's Well That Ends Well [Act II, sc. 3]

JULIET

It was the nightingale and not the lark,
That pierced the fearful hollow of thine ear;
Nightly she sings on
yon POMEGRANATE tree.

—Romeo and Juliet [Act III, sc. 5]

FRANCIS

Anon, anon, sir! Look down into the
*POMEGARNET, Ralph.

—Henry IV, Pt. 1 [Act II, sc. 4]

POPPY

IAGO

Not POPPY or mandragora,
Nor all the drowsy syrups of the world,
Shall ever medicine thee to that sweet sleep
Which thou ownedst yesterday.

—Othello [Act III, sc. 3]

POTATO

FALSTAFF

Let the sky rain POTATOES;
let it thunder to the tune of Greensleeves,
hail kissing-comfits,
and snow eringoes.

—Merry Wives of Windsor [Act V, sc. 5]

THERSITES

How the devil Luxury, with his fat rump and
POTATO-finger, tickles these together.

—Troilus and Cressida [Act V, sc. 2]

PRIMROSE

QUEEN

The violets, cowslips, and the PRIMROSES,
Bear to my closet.

—*Cymbeline* [Act I, sc. 5]

QUEEN MARGARET

I would be blind with weeping, sick with groans,
Look pale as PRIMROSE
with blood-drinking sighs,
And all to have the noble duke alive.

—*Henry VI, Pt. 2* [Act III, sc. 2]

ARVIRAGUS

Thou shalt not lack
The flower that's like thy face,
pale PRIMROSE...

—*Cymbeline* [Act IV, sc. 2]

HERMIA

In the wood where often you and I
Upon faint PRIMROSE-beds
were wont to lie.

—*A Midsummer Night's Dream* [Act I, sc. 1]

PERDITA

Pale PRIMROSES,
That die unmarried, ere they can behold
Bright Phœbus in his strength.

—*Winter's Tale* [Act IV, sc. 4]

OPHELIA

Like a puff'd and reckless libertine,
Himself the PRIMROSE path
of dalliance treads
And recks not his own rede.

—*Hamlet* [Act I, sc. 3]

PORTER

I had thought to have let in some of
all professions that go the PRIMROSE way
to the everlasting bonfire.

—*Macbeth* [Act II, sc. 3]

SONG [BOY]

PRIMROSE, first-born child of Ver
Merry spring-time's harbinger...

—*Two Noble Kinsmen* [Act I, sc. 1]

Witness this PRIMROSE bank whereon I lie.

—*Venus and Adonis*

QUINCE

NURSE

They call for dates and QUINCES
in the pastry.

—*Romeo and Juliet*
[Act IV, sc. 4]

RADISH

FALSTAFF

I do remember him at Clement's Inn
like a man made after supper of a cheese-paring:
when a' was naked, he was, for all the world,
like a forked RADISH,
with a head fantastically carved upon it.

—*Henry IV*, *Pt.* 2 [Act III, sc. 2]

FALSTAFF

If I fought not with fifty of them,
I am a bunch of RADISH.

—*Henry IV*, *Pt.* 1 [Act II, sc. 4]

REED

SECOND SERVANT

I had as lief have a REED
that will do me no service . . .

—Antony and Cleopatra [Act II, sc. 7]

ARIEL

His tears run down his beard, like winter's drops
From eaves of REEDS.

—Tempest [Act V, sc. 1]

ARIEL

With hair up-staring—
then like REEDS, not hair.

—Tempest [Act I, sc. 2]

HOTSPUR

Swift Severn's flood;
Who then, affrighted with their bloody looks,
Ran fearfully among the trembling REEDS.

—Henry IV, Pt. 1 [Act I, sc. 3]

WOOER

From the far shore—
thick set with REEDS and sedges . . .
I heard a voice, . . . yet perceived not
Who made the sound, the rushes and the REEDS
Had so encompassed it.

—Two Noble Kinsmen [Act IV, sc. 1]

PORTIA

And speak between the change of man and boy
With a REED voice.

—Merchant of Venice [Act III, sc. 4]

ARVIRAGUS

Fear no more the frown o' the great,
Thou art past the tyrant's stroke;
Care no more to clothe and eat;
To thee the REED is as the oak . . .

—Cymbeline [Act IV, sc. 2]

To Simois' REEDY banks the red blood ran.

—Lucrece

RHUBARB

MACBETH

What RHUBARB, cyme,
or what purgative drug
Would scour these English hence?

—*Macbeth* [Act V, sc. 3]

RICE

SHEPHERD'S SON / CLOWN

Let me see; what am I to buy for our
sheep-shearing feast? Three pound of sugar,
five pound of currants, RICE—
what will this sister of mine
do with RICE?

—*Winter's Tale* [Act IV, sc. 3]

ROSE

DIANA

When you have our ROSES,
You barely leave us thorns to prick ourselves
And mock us with our bareness.

—All's Well That Ends Well [Act IV, sc. 2]

HOTSPUR

To put down Richard, that sweet lovely ROSE,
And plant this thorn, this canker, Bolingbroke.

—Henry IV, Pt. 1 [Act I, sc. 3]

ROSES have THORNS
and silver fountains mud,
And loathsome canker lives in sweetest bud.

—Sonnet XXXV

SONG [PARSON EVANS]

There will we make our beds of ROSES
And a thousand fragrant posies.

—Merry Wives of Windsor [Act III, sc. 1]

OLIVIA

Cæsario, by the ROSES of the spring,
By maidhood, honour, truth, and everything,
I love thee . . .

—Twelfth Night [Act III, sc. 1]

The ROSE looks fair, but fairer we it deem
For that sweet odour that doth in it live.
The canker-blooms have full as deep a dye
As the perfumed tincture of the ROSES,
Hang on such THORNS,
and play as wantonly
When summer's breath
their masked buds discloses;
But, for their virtue only is their show,
They live unwoo'd and unrespected fade;
Die to themselves—sweet ROSES do not so;
Of their sweet deaths are sweetest odours made.

—Sonnet LIV

TITANIA

The seasons alter: hoary-headed frosts
Fall in the fresh lap of the CRIMSON ROSE.

—A Midsummer Night's Dream [Act II, sc. 1]

FLUTE / THISBE

Of colour like the RED ROSE
on triumphant brier.

—A Midsummer Night's Dream [Act III, sc. 1]

MISTRESS QUICKLY

Your colour, I warrant you,
is as RED AS ANY ROSE.

—Henry IV, Pt. 2 [Act II, sc. 4]

TYRRELL

Their lips were four RED ROSES on a stalk,
Which in their summer beauty
kiss'd each other.

—Richard III [Act IV, sc. 3]

More white and red than dove and ROSES are.

—Venus and Adonis

Nor did I wonder at the lily's white,
Nor praise the deep vermilion of the ROSE.

—Sonnet XCVIII

O how her fear did make her colour rise,
First red as ROSES that on lawn we lay,
Then white as lawn, the ROSES took away.

—Lucrece

Why should poor beauty indirectly seek
ROSES of shadow,
since his ROSE is true?

—Sonnet LXVII

BRUTUS

... Or veil'd dames
Commit the war of WHITE and DAMASK in
Their nicely-gawded cheeks to the wanton spoil
Of Phoebus' burning kisses.

—Coriolanus [Act II, sc. 1]

That beauty's ROSE might never die.

—Sonnet I

AUTOLYCUS

Gloves as sweet as DAMASK ROSES.

—*Winter's Tale* [Act IV, sc. 3]

WOOER

I'll bring a bevy,
A hundred black-eyed maids that love as I do,
With chaplets on their heads of daffadillies,
With cherry lips and cheeks of
DAMASK ROSES...

—*Two Noble Kinsmen* [Act IV, sc. 1]

BOYET

Blow like sweet ROSES in this summer air.

PRINCESS

How blow? how blow? Speak to be understood.

BOYET

Fair ladies mask'd are ROSES in their bud;
Dismask'd, their DAMASK
sweet commixture shown,
Are angels veiling clouds, or ROSES blown.

—*Love's Labour's Lost* [Act V, sc. 2]

PHEBE

A little riper and more lusty red
Than that mix'd in his cheek;
'twas just the difference
Between the CONSTANT RED and
MINGLED DAMASK.

—*As You Like It* [Act III, sc. 5]

I have seen ROSES DAMASK'd, red and white,
But no such ROSES see I in her cheeks.

—*Sonnet CXXX*

Nothing this wide universe I call
Save thou, my ROSE; in it thou art my all.

—*Sonnet CIX*

Who, when he lived, his breath and beauty set
Gloss on the ROSE, smell to the violet.

—*Venus and Adonis*

GOWER

Even her art sisters, the natural ROSES.

—*Pericles* [Act V, Chorus]

LORD

Let one attend him with a silver basin
Full of ROSE-WATER
and bestrew'd with flowers.

—*Taming of the Shrew* [Induction, sc. 1]

PETRUCHIO

I'll say she looks as clear
As morning ROSES
newly wash'd with dew.

—*Taming of the Shrew* [Act II, sc. 1]

FRIAR LAURENCE

The ROSES in thy lips and cheeks shall fade
To paly ashes.

—*Romeo and Juliet* [Act IV, sc. 1]

ROMEO

Remnants of packthread
and old CAKES OF ROSES
Were thinly scatter'd, to make up a show.

—*Romeo and Juliet* [Act V, sc. 1]

YORK

Then will I raise aloft
the MILK-WHITE ROSE,
With whose sweet smell the air shall be perfumed.

—*Henry VI, Pt. 2* [Act I, sc. 1]

QUEEN ISABEL

But soft, but see, or rather do not see,
My fair ROSE wither.

—*Richard II* [Act V, sc. 1]

OPHELIA

The expectancy and ROSE of the fair state.

—*Hamlet* [Act III, sc. 1]

What though the ROSE has prickles?
yet 'tis plucked.

—*Venus and Adonis*

JULIET

What's in a name? That which we call a ROSE
By any other name would smell as sweet.

—*Romeo and Juliet* [Act II, sc. 2]

CLEOPATRA

Against the blown ROSE
may they stop their nose
That kneel'd unto the buds.

—*Antony and Cleopatra* [Act III, sc. 13]

BOULT

For flesh and blood, sir, white and red, you
shall see a ROSE; and she were a ROSE indeed!

—*Pericles* [Act IV, sc. 6]

HAMLET

Such an act
That blurs the grace and blush of modesty,
Calls virtue hypocrite, takes off the ROSE
From the fair forehead of an innocent love,
And sets a blister there.

—*Hamlet* [Act III, sc. 4]

OTHELLO

Thou young and ROSE-lipp'd cherubim.

—*Othello* [Act IV, sc. 2]

TIMON

ROSE-cheeked youth.

—*Timon of Athens* [Act IV, sc. 3]

OTHELLO

When I have pluck'd the ROSE,
I cannot give it vital growth again,
It needs must wither. I'll smell it on the tree.

—*Othello* [Act V, sc. 2]

The ROSES fearfully in THORNS did stand,
One blushing shame, another white despair;
A third, nor red nor white, had stol'n of both
And to his robbery had annex'd thy breath.

—*Sonnet XCIX*

A sudden pale,
Like lawn being spread upon the blushing ROSE,
Usurps her cheek.

—*Venus and Adonis*

HAMLET

With two PROVINCIAL ROSES
on my razed shoes.

—*Hamlet* [Act III, sc. 2]

ORSINO

For women are as ROSES, whose fair flower
Being once display'd doth fall that very hour.

—Twelfth Night [Act II, sc. 4]

DON JOHN

I had rather be a canker in a hedge
than a ROSE in his grace.

—Much Ado About Nothing [Act I, sc. 3]

THESEUS

But earthlier happy is the ROSE distill'd
Than that which withering on the virgin thorn
Grows, lives, and dies in single blessedness.

—A Midsummer Night's Dream [Act I, sc. 1]

Their silent war of lilies and of ROSES.

—Lucrece

TITANIA

Some to kill cankers in the MUSK-ROSE buds.

—A Midsummer Night's Dream [Act II, sc. 3]

OBERON

Quite over-canopied with luscious woodbine,
With sweet MUSK-ROSES and with eglantine.

—A Midsummer Night's Dream [Act II, sc. 1]

TITANIA

Stick MUSK-ROSES in thy sleek, smooth head.

—A Midsummer Night's Dream [Act IV, sc. 1]

JULIA

The air hath starved the ROSES in her cheeks.

—Two Gentlemen of Verona [Act IV, sc. 4]

CONSTANCE

Of Nature's gifts,
thou may'st with lilies boast,
And with the half-blown ROSE.

—King John [Act III, sc. 1]

Shame, like a canker in the fragrant ROSE,
Doth spot the beauty of thy budding name.

—Sonnet XCV

BIRON

At Christmas I no more desire a ROSE
Than wish a snow in May's new-fangled mirth,
But like of each thing that in season grows.

—*Love's Labour's Lost* [Act I, sc. 1]

BASTARD

My face so thin,
That in mine ear I durst not
stick a ROSE.

—*King John* [Act I, sc. 1]

TOUCHSTONE

He that sweetest ROSE will find,
Must find Love's prick and Rosalind.

—*As You Like It* [Act III, sc. 2]

LYSANDER

How now, my love! Why is your cheek so pale?
How chance the ROSES there do fade so fast?

—*A Midsummer Night's Dream* [Act I, sc. 1]

KING FERDINAND

So sweet a kiss the golden sun gives not
To those fresh morning drops upon the ROSE.

—*Love's Labour's Lost* [Act IV, sc. 3]

ANTONY

Tell him he wears the ROSE
OF YOUTH upon him.

—*Antony and Cleopatra* [Act III, sc. 13]

LAERTES

O ROSE OF MAY,
Dear maid, kind sister, sweet Ophelia!

—*Hamlet* [Act IV, sc. 5]

SONG [BOY]

ROSES, their sharp spines being gone,
Not royal in their smells alone
But in their hue.

—*Two Noble Kinsmen* [Act I, sc. 1]

Glazed with crystal gate the glowing ROSES
That flame through water which their hue encloses.

—*A Lover's Complaint*

HENRY VI

Let me be umpire in this doubtful strife.
I see no reason, if I wear this ROSE
[*dons a red rose*]
That any one should therefore
be suspicious . . .

—*Henry VI, Pt.* 1 [Act 4, sc. 1]

RICHARD PLANTAGENET

I cannot rest
Until the WHITE ROSE that I wear be dyed
Even in the lukewarm blood of Henry's heart.

—*Henry VI, Pt.* 3 [Act I, sc. 5]

I know what THORNS
the growing ROSE defends.

—*Lucrece*

HENRY VI

The RED ROSE AND THE WHITE
are on his face,
The fatal colours of our striving houses:
The one his purple blood right well resembles;
The other his pale cheeks, methinks,
presenteth:
Wither one ROSE, and let the other flourish;
If you contend, a thousand lives must wither.

—*Henry VI, Pt.* 3 [Act II, sc. 5]

CLARENCE

Father of Warwick, know you what this means?
[*Taking his RED ROSE out of his hat*]
Look here, I throw my infamy at thee.

—*Henry VI, Pt.* 3 [Act V, sc. 1]

EMILIA

Of all flowers
Methinks a ROSE is best.

WOMAN

Why, gentle madam?

EMILIA

It is the very emblem of a maid.

—*Two Noble Kinsmen* [Act II, sc. 2]

That even for anger makes the Lily pale,
And the red ROSE blush at her own disgrace.

—*Lucrece*

RICHARD PLANTAGENET

From off this brier pluck
a WHITE ROSE with me.

SOMERSET

Pluck a RED ROSE from off this thorn with me.

WARWICK

I pluck this WHITE ROSE with Plantagenet.

SUFFOLK

I pluck this RED ROSE with young Somerset.

VERNON

The fewest ROSES are cropp'd
from the tree . . .

VERNON

I pluck this pale and maiden blossom here,
Giving my verdict on the WHITE ROSE side.

SOMERSET

Prick not your finger as you pluck it off,
Lest bleeding you do paint
the WHITE ROSE RED.

LAWYER

In sign whereof I pluck a WHITE ROSE too.

SOMERSET

Here in my scabbard, meditating that
Shall dye your WHITE ROSE
IN A BLOODY RED.

PLANTAGENET

Meantime your cheeks do
counterfeit our ROSES,
For pale they look with fear.

SOMERSET

'Tis not for fear but anger that thy cheeks
Blush for pure shame to counterfeit our ROSES.

PLANTAGENET

Hath not thy ROSE A CANKER, Somerset?

SOMERSET

Hath not thy ROSE A THORN, Plantagenet?

SOMERSET

Well, I'll find friends to wear
my BLEEDING ROSES.

PLANTAGENET

And, by my soul, this
PALE AND ANGRY ROSE,
As cognizance of my blood-drinking hate.

WARWICK

Will I upon thy party wear this ROSE.
And here I prophesy: this brawl to-day,
Grown to this faction in the Temple-garden,
Shall send between the RED ROSE
AND THE WHITE
A thousand souls to death and deadly night.

—*Henry VI, Pt.* 1 [Act 2, sc. 4]

RICHMOND

And then, as we have ta'en the sacrament,
We will unite the WHITE ROSE
AND THE RED:
Smile heaven upon this fair conjunction,
That long have frown'd upon their enmity!
What traitor hears me, and says not Amen?

—*Richard III* [Act V, sc. 5]

ROSEMARY

EDGAR

Bedlam beggars, who,
with roaring voices
Strike in their numb'd
and mortified bare arms
Pins, wooden pricks,
and sprigs of ROSEMARY.

—*King Lear* [Act II, sc. 3]

NURSE

Doth not ROSEMARY and Romeo
begin both with a letter?

ROMEO

Ay, nurse; what of that? both with an R.

NURSE

Ah, mocker! that's the dog's name;
R is for the—. No; I know it begins with some
other letter—and she hath the prettiest
sententious of it, of you and ROSEMARY,
that it would do you good to hear it.

—*Romeo and Juliet* [Act II, sc. 4]

OPHELIA

There's ROSEMARY, that's for
remembrance; pray, love, remember.

—*Hamlet* [Act IV, sc. 5]

PERDITA

For you there's ROSEMARY and rue;
these keep
Seeming and savour all the winter long;
Grace and remembrance be to you both.

—*Winter's Tale* [Act IV, sc. 4]

BAWD

Marry, come up, my dish of chastity with
ROSEMARY and bays.

—*Pericles* [Act IV, sc. 6]

FRIAR LAURENCE

Dry up your tears,
and stick your ROSEMARY
On this fair corse.

—*Romeo and Juliet* [Act IV, sc. 5]

RUE

Herb of Grace

PERDITA

For you there's rosemary and RUE;
these keep
Seeming and savour all the winter long;
GRACE and remembrance be to you both

—*Winter's Tale* [Act IV, sc. 4]

OPHELIA

There's RUE for you;
and here's some for me: we may call it HERB-
GRACE O' SUNDAYS:
O, you must wear your RUE with a difference.

—*Hamlet* [Act IV, sc. 5]

LAVATCH / CLOWN

Indeed, sir, she was the sweet marjoram of the
salad, or rather the HERB OF GRACE.

LAFEU

They are not salad-herbs, you knave,
they are nose-herbs.

—*All's Well That Ends Well* [Act IV, sc. 5]

GARDENER

Here did she fall a tear; here in this place
I'll set a bank of RUE, sour HERB OF GRACE:
RUE, even for ruth, here shortly shall be seen,
In the remembrance of a weeping queen.

—*Richard II* [Act III, sc. 4]

ANTONY

GRACE grow where these drops fall.

—*Antony and Cleopatra* [Act IV, sc. 2]

RUSH

*Rushes*Bulrush*

PHEBE

Lean but on a RUSH,
The cicatrice and capable impressure
Thy palm some moment keeps.

—*As You Like It* [Act III, sc. 5]

TITANIA

And never, since the middle summer's spring,
Met we on hill, in dale, forest or mead,
By paved fountain or by RUSHY brook,
Or in the beached margent of the sea.

—*A Midsummer Night's Dream* [Act II, sc. 1]

LAVATCH / CLOWN

As fit as Tib's RUSH for Tom's forefinger.

—*All's Well That Ends Well* [Act II, sc. 2]

ROMEO

Let wantons light of heart
Tickle the senseless RUSHES
with their heels.

—*Romeo and Juliet* [Act I, sc. 4]

ROSALIND

He taught me how to know a man in love;
in which cage of RUSHES
I am sure you are not prisoner.

—*As You Like It* [Act III, sc. 2]

DROMIO OF SYRACUSE

Some devils ask but the parings of one's nail,
A RUSH, a hair, a drop of blood, a pin,
A nut, a cherry-stone.

—*Comedy of Errors* [Act IV, sc. 3]

BASTARD

A RUSH will be a beam
To hang thee on.

—*King John* [Act IV, sc. 3]

FIRST GROOM

More RUSHES, more RUSHES.

—Henry IV, Pt. 2 [Act V, sc. 5]

EROS

He's walking in the garden—thus, and spurns
The RUSH that lies before him.

—Antony and Cleopatra [Act III, sc. 5]

OTHELLO

Man but a RUSH against Othello's breast,
    And he retires.

—Othello [Act V, sc. 2]

GRUMIO

Is supper ready, the house trimmed,
RUSHES strewed, cobwebs swept?

—Taming of the Shrew [Act IV, sc. 1]

KATHERINE

Be it moon or sun, or what you please,
    And if you please to call it
        a RUSH-CANDLE,
Henceforth I vow it shall be so for me.

—Taming of the Shrew [Act IV, sc. 5]

GLENDOWER

She bids you on the wanton RUSHES
    lay you down,
And rest your gentle head upon her lap.

—Henry IV, Pt. 1 [Act III, sc. 1]

MARCIUS

He that depends
Upon your favours swims with fins of lead
And hews down oaks with RUSHES.

—Coriolanus [Act I, sc. 1]

IACHIMO

Our Tarquin thus
Did softly press the RUSHES.

—Cymbeline [Act II, sc. 2]

FIRST SENATOR

Our gates
Which yet seem shut,
we have but pinn'd with RUSHES!
They'll open of themselves.

—Coriolanus [Act I, sc. 4]

And being lighted, by the light he spies
Lucretia's glove, wherein her needle sticks;
He takes it from the RUSHES where it lies.

—Lucrece

WOOER

Rings she made
Of RUSHES that grew by, and to 'em spoke
The prettiest posies.

—Two Noble Kinsmen [Act IV, sc. 1]

WOOER

Her careless tresses
A wreake of BULRUSH rounded.

—Two Noble Kinsmen [Act IV, sc. 1]

RYE

IRIS

Ceres, most bounteous lady,
thy rich leas
Of wheat, RYE, barley,
vetches, oats, and pease.

—*Tempest* [Act IV, sc. 1]

IRIS

You sunburnt sicklemen,
of August weary,
Come hither from the furrow
and be merry;
Make holiday;
your RYE-straw hats put on.

—*Tempest* [Act IV, sc. 1]

SONG [1ST / 2ND PAGE]

Between the acres of the RYE
These pretty country folks would lye.

—*As You Like It* [Act V, sc. 3]

SAFFRON

CERES

Who, with thy SAFFRON wings
upon my flowers,
Diffusest honeydrops, refreshing showers.

—Tempest [Act IV, sc. 1]

ANTIPHOLUS OF EPHESUS

Did this companion
with the SAFFRON face
Revel and feast it at my house to day?

—Comedy of Errors [Act IV, sc. 4]

SHEPHERD'S SON / CLOWN

I must have SAFFRON
to colour the Warden pies.

—Winter's Tale [Act IV, sc. 3]

LAFEU

No, no, no, your son was misled
with a snipt-taffeta fellow there,
whose villanous SAFFRON would
have made all the unbaked and doughy
youth of a nation in his colour.

—All's Well That Ends Well [Act IV, sc. 5]

SAMPHIRE

EDGAR

Half-way down
Hangs one that gathers
SAMPHIRE, dreadful trade!
Methinks he seems no bigger than his head.

—*King Lear* [Act IV, sc. 6]

SAVORY

PERDITA

Here's flowers for you;
Hot lavender, mints, SAVORY,
marjoram.

—*Winter's Tale* [Act IV, sc. 4]

SEDGE

SECOND SERVANT

And Cytherea all in SEDGES hid,
Which seem to move and wanton with her breath,
Even as the waving SEDGES play with wind.

—Taming of the Shrew [Induction, sc. 2]

IRIS

You nymphs, called Naiads, of the winding brooks,
With your SEDGED crowns
and ever-harmless looks.

—Tempest [Act IV, sc. 1]

JULIA

He makes sweet music with the enamell'd stones,
Giving a gentle kiss to every SEDGE
He overtaketh in his pilgrimage . . .

—Two Gentlemen of Verona [Act II, sc. 7]

BENEDICK

Alas, poor hurt fowl! now will
he creep into SEDGES.

—Much Ado About Nothing [Act II, sc. 1]

HOTSPUR

The gentle Severn's SEDGY bank.

—Henry IV, Pt. 1 [Act I, sc. 3]

SPEAR-GRASS

BARDOLPH

... to tickle our noses with SPEAR-GRASS to make them bleed, and then to beslubber our garments with it and swear it was the blood of true men.

—Henry IV, Pt. I [Act II, sc. 4]

STRAWBERRY

GLOUCESTER

My Lord of Ely, when I was last in Holborn,
I saw good STRAWBERRIES
in your garden there;
I do beseech you send for some of them.

ELY

Marry, and will, my Lord,
with all my heart....
Where is my lord Protector? I have sent
For these STRAWBERRIES.

—*Richard III* [Act III, sc. 4]

IAGO

Have you not sometimes seen a handkerchief
Spotted with STRAWBERRIES
in your wife's hand?

—*Othello* [Act III, sc. 3]

BISHOP OF ELY

The STRAWBERRY grows
underneath the nettle,
And wholesome berries thrive and ripen best
Neighbour'd by fruit of baser quality;

—*Henry V* [Act I, sc. 1]

SUGAR

PRINCE HENRY

But, sweet Ned—to sweeten which name of Ned,
I give thee this pennyworth of SUGAR, clapped
even now into my hand by an under-skinker....
To drive away the time till Falstaff comes,
I prithee, do thou stand in some by-room,
while I question my puny Drawer to what
end he gave me the SUGAR....
Nay, but hark you, Francis;
for the SUGAR thou gavest me,
'twas a pennyworth, was't not?

—Henry IV, Pt. 1 [Act II, sc. 4]

BIRON

White-handed mistress,
one sweet word with thee.

PRINCESS OF FRANCE

Honey, and milk, and SUGAR,
there is three.

—Love's Labour's Lost [Act V, sc. 2]

MISTRESS QUICKLY

And in such wine and SUGAR
of the best and the fairest,
that would have won any woman's heart.

—Merry Wives of Windsor [Act II, sc. 2]

BASSANIO

Here are sever'd lips
Parted with SUGAR breath; so sweet a bar
Should sunder such sweet friends.

—*Merchant of Venice*
[Act III, sc. 2]

NORTHUMBERLAND

Your fair discourse hath been as SUGAR,
Making the hard way sweet and delectable.

—*Richard II* [Act II, sc. 3]

SHEPHERD'S SON / CLOWN

Let me see—what am I to buy for our
sheep-shearing feast? Three pound of SUGAR,
five pound of currants.

—*Winter's Tale* [Act IV, sc. 3]

HENRY V

You have witchcraft in your lips, Kate:
there is more eloquence
in a SUGAR touch of them
than in the tongues of the French council.

—*Henry V* [Act V, sc. 2]

TOUCHSTONE

Honesty coupled to beauty
is to have honey a sauce to SUGAR.

—*As You Like It* [Act III, sc. 2]

QUEEN MARGARET

Poor painted Queen, vain flourish of my fortune!
Why strew'st thou SUGAR
on that bottled spider
Whose deadly web ensnareth thee about?

—*Richard III* [Act I, sc. 3]

POLONIUS

We are oft to blame in this—
Tis too much proved—that with
devotion's visage
And pious actions we do SUGAR o'er
The devil himself.

—*Hamlet* [Act III, sc. 1]

BRABANTIO

These sentences, to SUGAR, or to gall,
Being strong on both sides, are equivocal.

—*Othello* [Act I, sc. 3]

POINS

What says Sir John Sack and SUGAR?

—*Henry IV, Pt.* 1 [Act I, sc. 2]

Thy SUGAR'D tongue
to bitter wormwood taste.

—*Lucrece*

SYCAMORE

BENVOLIO

Underneath the grove of SYCAMORE
That westward rooteth from this city side,
So early walking did I see your son.

—*Romeo and Juliet* [Act I, sc. 1]

DESDEMONA [SINGING]

The poor soul sat sighing
by a SYCAMORE tree.

—*Othello* [Act IV, sc. 3]

BOYET

Under the cool shade of a SYCAMORE
I thought to close mine eyes some half an hour.

—*Love's Labour's Lost* [Act V, sc. 2]

THISTLE

BURGUNDY

And nothing teems
But hateful docks, rough THISTLES,
kecksies, burs.

—*Henry V* [Act V, sc. 2]

BOTTOM

Mounsieur Cobweb, good Mounsieur,
get you your weapons ready in your hand,
and kill me a red-hipped humble bee
on the top of a THISTLE; and, good
Mounsieur, bring me the honey-bag.

—*A Midsummer Night's Dream* [Act IV, sc. 1]

THORNS

ARIEL

Tooth'd briers, sharp furzes, pricking goss,
and THORNS,
Which entered their frail shins.

—*Tempest* [Act IV, sc. 1]

HELENA

When briers shall have leaves
as well as THORNS,
And be as sweet as sharp.

—*All's Well That Ends Well* [Act IV, sc. 4]

PETER QUINCE

One must come in with a bush of THORNS
and a lanthorn, and say he comes in to disfigure,
or to present, the person of Moonshine.

—*A Midsummer Night's Dream* [Act III, sc. 1]

PUCK

For briers and THORNS
at their apparel snatch.

—*A Midsummer Night's Dream* [Act III, sc. 2]

PROLOGUE / PETER QUINCE

This man with lanthorn, dog,
and bush of THORN,
Presenteth Moonshine.

—*A Midsummer Night's Dream* [Act V, sc. 1]

MOONSHINE / STARVELING

All that I have to say, is to tell you that the lanthorn
is the moon; I, the man in the moon; this THORN-
BUSH my THORN-BUSH; and this dog my dog.

—*A Midsummer Night's Dream* [Act V, sc. 1]

DUMAIN

But, alack, my hand is sworn
Ne'er to pluck thee from thy THORN.

—*Love's Labour's Lost* [Act IV, sc. 3]

BISHOP OF CARLISLE

The woe's to come; the children yet unborn
Shall feel this day as sharp to them as THORN.

—*Richard II* [Act IV, sc. 1]

HENRY VI

The care you have of us,
To mow down THORNS
that would annoy our foot,
Is worthy praise.

—*Henry VI, Pt. 2* [Act III, sc. 1]

GLOUCESTER

And I—like one lost in a THORNY wood,
That rends the THORNS
and is rent with the THORNS,
Seeking a way, and straying from the way.

—*Henry VI, Pt. 3* [Act III, sc. 2]

173

EDWARD IV

Brave followers, yonder stands
the THORNY wood.

—*Henry VI, Pt. 3* [Act V, sc. 4]

EDWARD IV

What! can so young a THORN begin to prick.

—*Henry VI, Pt. 3* [Act V, sc. 5]

ROMEO

Is love a tender thing? It is too rough,
Too rude, too boisterous,
and it pricks like THORN.

—*Romeo and Juliet* [Act I, sc. 4]

BOULT

A THORNIER piece of ground.

—*Pericles* [Act IV, sc. 6]

LEONTES

Which being spotted
Is goads, THORNS, nettles, tails of wasps.

—*Winter's Tale* [Act I, sc. 2]

FLORIZEL

But O, the THORNS we stand upon!

—*Winter's Tale* [Act IV, sc. 4]

OPHELIA

Do not, as some ungracious pastors do,
Shew me the steep
and THORNY path to Heaven.

—*Hamlet* [Act I, sc. 3]

GHOST

Leave her to Heaven,
And to those THORNS that in her bosom lodge,
To prick and sting her.

—*Hamlet* [Act I, sc. 5]

BASTARD

I am amazed, methinks, and lose my way
Among the THORNS and dangers of this world.

—*King John* [Act IV, sc. 3]

COUNTESS OF ROUSILLION

This THORN
Doth to our rose of youth rightly belong.

—*All's Well That Ends Well* [Act I, sc. 3]

DIANA

You barely leave our THORNS to prick ourselves
And mock us with our bareness.

—*All's Well That Ends Well* [Act IV, sc. 2]

And whiles against a THORN
thou bear'st thy part
To keep thy sharp woes waking, wretched I . . .

—*Lucrece*

THYME

OBERON

I know a bank where the wild THYME blows . . .

—*A Midsummer Night's Dream* [Act II, sc. 1]

IAGO

We will plant nettles or sow lettuce,
set hyssop and weed up THYME.

—*Othello* [Act I, sc. 3]

SONG [BOY]

But in their hue;
Maiden pinks, of odor faint,
Daisies, smell-less yet most quaint,
And sweet THYME true.

—*Two Noble Kinsmen* [Act I, sc. 1]

TURNIP

ANNE PAGE

Alas! I had rather be set quick i' the earth
And boul'd to death with TURNIPS.

—*Merry Wives of Windsor* [Act III, sc. 4]

VINE

[*see also Grapes**]

SONG

Come, thou monarch of the VINE,
Plumpy Bacchus, with pink eyne!
In thy fats our cares be drown'd,
With thy GRAPES our hairs be crown'd.

—*Antony and Cleopatra* [Act II, sc. 7]

TIMON

Dry up thy marrows, VINES,
and plough-torn leas.

—*Timon of Athens* [Act IV, sc. 3]

BURGUNDY

Her VINE, the merry cheerer of the heart,
Unpruned, dies.
Our vineyards, fallows, meads, and hedges,
Defective in their natures, grow to wildness.

—*Henry V* [Act V, sc. 2]

MORTIMER

And pithless arms, like to a wither'd VINE
That droops his sapless branches to the ground.

—*Henry VI, Pt.* 1 [Act II, sc. 5]

CRANMER

In her days every man shall eat in safety,
Under his own VINE, what he plants; and sing
The merry songs of peace to all his neighbours.

—*Henry VIII* [Act V, sc. 5]

CRANMER

Peace, plenty, love, truth, terror,
That were the servants to this chosen infant,
Shall then be his,
and like a VINE grow to him.

—*Henry VIII* [Act V, sc. 5]

KING LEAR

Now, our joy,
Although the last, not least; to whose young love
The VINES of France and milk of Burgundy
Strive to be interess'd.

—*King Lear* [Act I, sc. 1]

ARVIRAGUS

And let the stinking elder, grief, untwine
His perishing root with the increasing VINE!

—*Cymbeline* [Act IV, sc. 2]

ADRIANA

Thou art an elm, my husband, I a VINE,
Whose weakness married to thy stronger state
Makes me with thy strength to communicate.

—Comedy of Errors [Act II, sc. 2]

CERES

VINES with clustering bunches growing,
Plants with goodly burthen bowing.

—Tempest [Act IV, sc. 1]

RICHMOND

Usurping boar,
That spoil'd your summer fields
and fruitful VINES.

—Richard III [Act V, sc. 2]

ARCITE

The VINE shall grow, but we shall never see it.

—Two Noble Kinsmen [Act II, sc. 2]

For one sweet GRAPE,
who will the VINE destroy?

—Lucrece

VIOLET

OBERON

Where oxlips and the nodding VIOLET grows.

—*A Midsummer Night's Dream* [Act II, sc. 1]

QUEEN

The VIOLETS, cowslips, and the primroses,
Bear to my closet.

—*Cymbeline* [Act I, sc. 5]

SALISBURY

To gild refined gold, to paint the lily,
To throw a perfume on the VIOLET . . .
Is wasteful and ridiculous excess.

—*King John* [Act IV, sc. 2]

ANGELO

It is I,
That, lying by the VIOLET in the sun,
Do as the carrion does,
not as the flower,
Corrupt with virtuous season.

—*Measure for Measure* [Act II, sc. 2]

HENRY V

I think the king is but a man, as I am; the
VIOLET smells to him as it doth to me.

—*Henry V* [Act IV, sc. 1]

LAERTES

A VIOLET in the youth of primy nature,
Forward, not permanent; sweet, not lasting.
The perfume and suppliance of a minute;
No more.

—*Hamlet* [Act I, sc. 3]

OPHELIA

I would give you some VIOLETS,
but they withered all when my father died.

—Hamlet [Act IV, sc. 5]

LAERTES

Lay her i' the earth,
And from her fair and unpolluted flesh
May VIOLETS spring!

—Hamlet [Act V, sc. 1]

BELARIUS

They are as gentle
As zephyrs blowing below the VIOLET . . .

—Cymbeline [Act IV, sc. 2]

ORSINO

It came o'er my ear like the sweet sound,
That breathes upon a bank of VIOLETS . . .

—Twelfth Night [Act I, sc. 1]

SONG OF SPRING

When daisies pied, and VIOLETS blue . . .

—Love's Labour's Lost [Act V, sc. 2]

PERDITA

VIOLETS dim,
But sweeter than the lids of Juno's eyes
Or Cytherea's breath.

—Winter's Tale [Act IV, sc. 4]

DUCHESS OF YORK

Welcome, my son; who are the VIOLETS now,
That strew the green lap of the new-come spring?

—Richard II [Act V, sc. 2]

MARINA

The yellows, blues,
The purple VIOLETS and marigolds,
Shall as a carpet hang upon thy grave
While summer-days do last.

—Pericles [Act IV, sc. 1]

These blue-veined VIOLETS whereon we lean
Never can blab, nor know not what we mean.

—Venus and Adonis

Who when he lived, his breath and beauty set
Gloss on the rose, smell to the VIOLET.

—Venus and Adonis

When I behold the VIOLET past prime,
And sable curls all silver'd o'er with white,
Then of thy beauty do I question make,
That thou among the wastes of time must go . . .

—Sonnet XII

The forward VIOLET thus did I chide:
"Sweet thief, whence didst thou
steal thy sweet that smells,
If not from my love's breath? The purple pride
Which on thy soft cheek for complexion dwells
In my love's veins thou hast too grossly died."

—Sonnet XCIX

WALNUT

PETRUCHIO

Why, 'tis a cockle or a WALNUT-shell,
A knack, a toy, a trick, a baby's cap.

—*Taming of the Shrew* [Act IV, sc. 3]

MASTER FORD

Let them say of me, "As jealous as Ford
that searched a hollow WALNUT
for his wife's leman."

—*Merry Wives of Windsor* [Act IV, sc. 2]

WHEAT / VETCHES

Stubble [*see also CORN*]*

IRIS

Ceres, most bounteous lady, thy rich leas
Of WHEAT, rye, barley,
VETCHES, oats, and pease.

—*Tempest* [Act IV, sc. 1]

BASSANIO

His reasons are as two grains of WHEAT hid
in two bushels of CHAFF; you shall seek
all day ere you find them, and when you have
them, they are not worth the search.

—*Merchant of Venice* [Act I, sc. 1]

HAMLET

As peace should still
her WHEATEN garland wear.

—*Hamlet* [Act V, sc. 2]

DAVY

And again, sir,
shall we sow the headland
with WHEAT?

SHALLOW

With RED WHEAT, Davy.

—*Henry IV, Pt. 2* [Act V, sc. 1]

POMPEY

To send measures of WHEAT to Rome.

—*Antony and Cleopatra* [Act II, sc. 6]

EDGAR

This is the foul fiend Flibbertigibbet. . . .
He mildews the WHITE WHEAT, and hurts
the poor creatures of earth.

—*King Lear* [Act III, sc. 4]

HELENA

More tuneable than lark to shepherd's ear,
When WHEAT IS GREEN,
when hawthorn-buds appear.

—*A Midsummer Night's Dream* [Act I, sc. 1]

PANDARUS

He that will have a cake out of the WHEAT,
must needs tarry the grinding.

—*Troilus and Cressida* [Act I, sc. 1]

THESEUS

Your WHEATEN wreathe
Was then nor threashed
nor blasted.

—*Two Noble Kinsmen*
[Act I, sc. 1]

SICINIUS

To kindle
their dry STUBBLE;
and their blaze
Shall darken him
for ever.

—*Coriolanus*
[Act II, sc. 1]

HOTSPUR

Came there a certain lord, neat,
and trimly dress'd,
Fresh as a bridegroom;
and his chin new reap'd
Show'd like a STUBBLE-land
at harvest-home . . .

—*Henry IV, Pt. 1* [Act I, sc. 3]

WILLOW

Osier

BENEDICK

I offered him my company to a WILLOW tree,
either to make him a garland,
as being forsaken, or to bind him up a rod,
as being worthy to be whipped.

—*Much Ado About Nothing* [Act II, sc. 1]

NATHANIEL

These thoughts to me were oaks,
to thee like OSIERS bow'd.

—*Love's Labour's Lost* [Act IV, sc. 2]

LORENZO

In such a night
Stood Dido, with a WILLOW in her hand,
Upon the wild sea-banks.

—*Merchant of Venice* [Act V, sc. 1]

FRIAR LAURENCE

I must up-fill this OSIER cage of ours
With baleful weeds
and precious-juiced flowers.

—*Romeo and Juliet* [Act II, sc. 3]

CELIA

The rank of OSIERS by the murmuring stream
Left on your right hand, brings you to the place.

—*As You Like It* [Act IV, sc. 3]

DESDEMONA [SINGING]

The poor soul sat sighing by a Sycamore tree.
Sing all a green WILLOW;
Her hand on her bosom, her head on her knee,
Sing WILLOW, WILLOW, WILLOW.
The fresh streams ran by her,
and murmur'd her moans;
Sing WILLOW, WILLOW, WILLOW.
Her salt tears fell from her and soften'd the stones,
Sing WILLOW, WILLOW, WILLOW.
Sing all a green WILLOW must be my garland.

—*Othello* [Act IV, sc. 3]

GERTRUDE

There is a WILLOW grows aslant a brook
That shows his hoar leaves in the glassy stream;
There with fantastic garlands did she come
Of crow-flowers, nettles, daisies, and long purples
That liberal shepherds give a grosser name,
But our cold maids do dead men's fingers call:
There, on the pendent boughs her coronet weeds
Clambering to hang, an envious sliver broke . . .

—Hamlet [Act IV, sc. 7]

EMILIA

I will play the swan,
And die in music. [*sings*]
WILLOW, WILLOW, WILLOW.

—Othello [Act V, sc. 2]

WOOER

Then she sang
Nothing but WILLOW, WILLOW, WILLOW.

—Two Noble Kinsmen [Act IV, sc. 1]

BONA

Tell him, in hope he'll prove a widower shortly,
I'll wear the WILLOW garland for his sake.

—Henry VI, Pt. 3 [Act III, sc. 3]

POST

[He repeats her words in a report.]

—Henry VI, Pt. 3 [Act IV, sc. 1]

VIOLA

Make me a WILLOW cabin
at your gate.

—Twelfth Night [Act I, sc. 5]

BENEDICK

Come, will you go with me?

CLAUDIO

Whither?

BENEDICK

Even to the next WILLOW,
about your own business.

—Much Ado About Nothing [Act II, sc. 1]

Though to myself forsworn,
to thee I'll constant prove;
Those thoughts, to me like oaks,
to thee like OSIERS bow'd.

—Passionate Pilgrim

WORMWOOD

Dian's Bud

OBERON

Be, as thou wast wont to be,
See, as thou wast wont to see;
DIAN'S BUD o'er Cupid's flower
Hath such force and blessed power.

—*A Midsummer Night's Dream* [Act IV, sc. 1]

NURSE

For I had then laid
WORMWOOD to my dug.
Sitting in the sun
under the dove-house wall;
... as I said,
when it did taste
the WORMWOOD
on the nipple
Of my dug, and felt it bitter,
pretty fool ...

—*Romeo and Juliet* [Act I, sc. 3]

Thy secret pleasure turns to open shame,
Thy private feasting to a public fast,
Thy smoothing titles to a ragged name,
Thy sugar'd tongue
to bitter WORMWOOD taste.

—*Lucrece*

HAMLET

[aside] WORMWOOD, WORMWOOD.

—*Hamlet* [Act III, sc. 2]

ROSALINE

To weed this WORMWOOD
from your fruitful brain.

—*Love's Labour's Lost* [Act V, sc. 2]

YEW

SONG [FESTE]

My shroud of white, stuck all with YEW,
O, prepare it.

—*Twelfth Night* [Act II, sc. 4]

SCROOP

Thy very beadsmen learn to bend their bows
Of double-fatal YEW against thy state.

—*Richard II* [Act III, sc. 2]

TAMORA

But straight they told me they would bind me here
Unto the body of a dismal YEW,
And leave me to this miserable death.

—*Titus Andronicus* [Act II, sc. 3]

PARIS

Under yond YEW-trees lay thee all along,
Holding thine ear close to the hollow ground;
So shall no foot upon the churchyard tread
[Being loose, unfirm, with digging up of graves]
But thou shalt hear it.

—*Romeo and Juliet*
[Act V, sc. 3]

BALTHASAR

As I did sleep under this YEW tree here,
I dreamt my master and another fought,
And that my master slew him.

—*Romeo and Juliet* [Act V, sc. 3]

THIRD WITCH

Gall of goat, and slips of YEW
Sliver'd in the moon's eclipse.

—*Macbeth* [Act IV, sc. 1]

❧ BOTANICALS DEFINED ❧

Syllabic Sketches

A

ACONITUM – Aconite, a.k.a. Wolfs-bane, Monkshood, Devil's Helmet, and Queen of All Poisons—although other poisons might resent that hyperbole [*see* HEBENON/HEBONA]. But most of the 250-plus species in this genus are highly toxic. It's pretty enough to grace gardens, and can be employed for antidotal purposes, but it's most appreciated as a narcotic. A staple for witches and a stealth poison in antique wars, it may also be what tipped Laertes' sword, given that its possible root is the word *akon,* meaning dart or javelin in Greek. It also gets a shout-out in Ovid's *Metamorphoses,* Shakespeare's favorite book.

ACORN – Fruit of the OAK tree; the leathery outer nut/seed is cradled in a *cupule* [cup]. The acorn can represent the weak and insignificant offspring of its mighty Oak progenitor; conversely, it is also the seed of inherent potential for the same mighty attributes. MAST was a term for fallen acorns, a prized find of foraging pigs.

ADONIS FLOWER/ FRITILLARY – This flower has puzzled scholars for centuries, but why? The anemone in Ovid's original tale of Venus and Adonis was assumed to be in Shakespeare's poem [even though he always puts his own spin on his source material], but the "purple flower . . . chequer'd with white" that springs from dead Adonis's

blood defies that description. It does, however, perfectly fit the *Fritillaria meleagris,* a.k.a. Snakeshead Fritillary, or Turkie flower [so named by Flemish botanist Rembert Dodoens given the similar pattern on guinea fowl, called turkeys in England at that time]. Apothecary Noël Caperon imported the sample c. 1570 from Orleans, France, modestly calling it *Narcissus caperonius;* John Gerard, author of the *Herball,* became a fan of the flower, dubbing it the Checkered Daffodil, and he put it on the cover of his 1597 tome—so there it was, in a contemporaneous source all along, easily identifiable.

ALMOND – The almond tree, a prized cultivar first recorded in the mid-sixteenth century, arrived almost concurrent with wealthy Elizabethans' growing passion for sugar, which, mixed with rose water and the sweet nut, made marzipan ["marchpane" in *Romeo and Juliet*], a fashionable confection. Parrots apparently found the nut irresistible, which speaks to the sense of Thersites' line; the proverbial phrase is echoed in Shakespeare contemporary Thomas Nashe's *An Almond for a Parrot,* and in Ben Jonson's *The Magnetick Lady* some years later.

ALOE – Nowadays this succulent plant is considered synonymous with a soothing salve, but the one referenced in Shakespeare, although still medicinal, is a bitter

version—originally imported from India or Asia—a strong purgative with an intense fragrance.

APPLE – Among the earliest cultivated fruit trees, apples were both medicinal and edible, though the term *apple* could be applied generically to other fruits as well. In addition to sustenance, Shakespeare finds the apple ripe for metaphor. Specific types he mentions:

> ⌖ **APPLE-JOHN** – a long-lasting apple that looks worn or old.

> ⌖ **BITTER-SWEETING** – a sweetish variety, possibly a cider apple or one used in cookery.

> ⌖ **CODLING** – an immature apple, unripe.

> ⌖ **PIPPIN** – an oblong, long-lasting apple usually raised from pips [individual roots].

> ⌖ **POMEWATER** – a largish, tart, juicy, pale-skinned apple.

> ⌖ **LEATHER-COAT** – this has come to be known as a Golden Russet, a medium-size apple with a sharp/ sweet flavor and crisp bite; cataloged among the best apple trees. However, since

Shakespeare seems to be the first mention, the context indicates that he is actually referring to the Caraways themselves and their "seed" casings, so the quote has been moved to CARAWAY

⌐ COSTARD – the name of a comic character in *Love's Labour's Lost,* the word itself also an antique term for *Apple,* usually oversize, leading to its double meaning, a head. Hence, the rustic name for an apple seller became *costardmonger,* elided and morphed into *costermonger/s* —a vagabond subculture of fruit sellers with a rowdy, low, and lawless reputation [the term was also occasionally applied to actors].

ANGELICA – The plant, pictured in the Introduction, is named as a character in *Romeo and Juliet.* Speculation runs the gamut on this garden and wild herb: a kitchen wench, the first name of the Nurse, an "antidote" of sorts

to Juliet's previously mentioned mandrake, a sweetmeat to contrast with the baked meats being prepared for the wedding feast . . . Interestingly, contemporary writer Robert Greene has a silent, single-mentioned character called Angelica in his *Perimedes.*

APRICOT – *Apricock* in Shakespeare's day, a derivation of *Abrecox/Aprecox* from the original Latin [*præcox/præcoquus*], the fruit may have arrived in England c. Henry VIII's reign via Italy, Spain, or the Silk Road from China. It was considered a fruit of the wealthy, and earned the nickname precocious tree [another echo of the Latin] by blooming earlier than the PEACH. That it appears in *Richard II* is considered a time line anomaly [unless Shakespeare knew something we don't yet and it immigrated earlier, perhaps during the Roman occupation].

ARABIAN TREE [ACACIA] – Many scholars have assumed the tree Othello is talking about is the PALM or

Myrrh [whose gum has medicinal applications but not for eyes], but sixteenth-century herbals, including Gerard's, draw stronger connections with the *gummi arabicum* of the Acacia or Aegyptian Thorne, in relation to eye treatments; a thirteenth-century Italian surgeon referenced its gum specifically as tears. The tree referred to in both *Tempest* and *Phoenix and the Turtle,* however, is likely the PALM, which was believed to house the mythical phoenix, hence its eventual botanic name: *Phoenix dactylifera.*

ASH – An English timber tree renowned for fast growth and strength; a staple for reliable tools and spears. Shakespeare's sole use of the close-grained wood cited as splintering against Coriolanus speaks to his superior strength.

ASPEN – In the poplar genus, distinguished by the flat stems [as opposed to round] that attach Aspen leaves to the tree, which cause the perpetual motion, as if they are always quivering.

B

BACHELOR'S BUTTONS/BUDS – A popular name for plants with button-like buds and flowers. Carried in men's pockets, tucked in ladies' plackets, or secreted in other folds of clothing, arrays of sweet-smelling buds were employed to mask personal odor and to create pleasant "airs" and positive memories of courtiers' time together. As talismans, these flowers could indicate the success or failure of the courting ritual based on their retention, or loss, of freshness. The

Bachelor's Button eventually migrated to the lapel or buttonhole.

BALM, BALSAM and BALSAMUM – The soothing application of these plants ultimately became synonymous with succor in general. Using generous parameters, we only included quotes referencing the plants [as opposed to metaphor, e.g., *balm of my poor eyes* = tears]. Balm was probably Lemon Balm, with its delicate, sweet scent, used as a salve for wounds and similar

medicaments. It was often used interchangeably with Balsam and Balsamum, varieties of gum-bearing trees [we illustrate BALM and BALSAMUM]; all were used to make healing unguents, but also for purposes such as embalming a revered corpse or anointing a sovereign.

BARLEY – A grain crop considered inferior to WHEAT for bread making, but a staple in times of shortage. Also used for brewing [*bar-ley* means beer plant]. It is suggested that the "barley-broth" disdained by the French constable in the quote from *Henry V* is as much about the medicinal broth [to cool the blood] as it is a sneering reference to English beer.

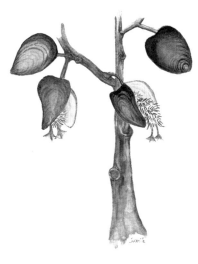

BARNACLE – Caliban in *The Tempest*'s fears "We shall . . . all be turn'd to Barnacles." Although the crustaceans that stick to the bottom of boats might be a good guess for these island-dwellers, 16th c. Barnacles were *firmly* believed to be geese that grew from the "Barnacle tree, or the tree bearing Geese" [John Gerard swears to have seen them in person]. The legendary tree seems to have been grafted from sea fables and a 14th c. traveler's tale. There are however Barnacle geese today, born from a traditional mother goose.

BAY TREE/LAUREL – A favorite of Delphic priestesses and the god Apollo, the glossy evergreen leaves of Sweet Bay [*Laurus nobilis*] have long been associated with royalty, immortality, and crowns of victory in war. An Italian superstition cites them as

harbingers of calamity in a country if they wither and die.

BEANS – Pulses [the seeds of some kinds of leguminous plants] or beans seem to suffer from a low reputation in Shakespeare [one writer dubbed them unromantic]. Usually some type of broad bean used for horse feed [which when damp caused intestinal upset] or food only fit for the common or poor folk.

BILBERRY – Growing on a common shrub found on mossy heaths or in thickets, these wild berries, a.k.a. whortleberries, heath-berries, or whinberries, are known for the dark blue stain they leave on lips and fingers, hence Pistol's line about pinching the ladies till they were bruised the color of the fruit. They only make a solo appearance in Shakespeare, although their wild state suggests they might also be the berries mentioned in *Timon* and *Titus*.

BIRCH – This native tree gets short shrift in Shakespeare; the two mentions skip its graceful mien in favor of the use of its branches, dried twigs bound together to discipline children, giving rise to the term *birching*. Also used on wives and by witches.

BLACKBERRIES/ BRAMBLES – Another candidate for the berries noted in *Titus* and *Timon*, these wild berries are mentioned for their common availability both as easily edible and as thorny inhibitors in underbrush.

BOX TREE – Because of its ubiquity as a hedge plant easily clipped into all manner of topiary for knot gardens, great gardens, arbors, and more, it's not surprising

that Box pops up in Olivia's garden as a hiding place for Malvolio's malefactors.

BRIERS – The prickly spires on rose stems, or any "tooth'd" and thorny aspects of a plant—a variety of options are considered Briers; we've illustrated a Scotch Rose as the generic Brier Rose, alongside a Blackberry bramble, but Hawthorn brakes and other sharp, spiky botanical elements qualify as the rough underside of nature's sylvan beauty. *See also* THORNS.

BROOM – This flowering shrub holds both a lowly and a [secretly] lofty place in Shakespeare. Native to heaths, the sweetly scented, bright golden blossoms get only one shout-out as flowers in *Tempest;* Puck's mention in its sweeping capacity is included because, as a sprite, he could still be using the pretty plant rather than its more prosaic household form [a reference to the broomstick as utilitarian tool is omitted]. But, from its antique Latin designation, *Planta genista,* comes Plantagenet, the name of the prominent family of British royalty [in six of Shakespeare's History plays], including Richard Plantagenet a.k.a. Richard III of car park fame [locating his skeleton in a local Leicester parking lot has been the find of the century for some British historians].

BULRUSH – *see* RUSHES.

BURDOCK/HARDOCK/ HARLOCK/CHARLOCK/ HARDOKE and BUR/ BURRES – Although Cordelia speaks disparagingly of this weed [in multitudinous spellings!], it can be quite fetching in its native habitat [and used to dye hair red]. But the dried-up, unopened flower head becomes the clinging Burr, whose long, stiff bracts, with hooked tips, stick steadfastly to anything nearby;

BURNET – In the Rose family, a.k.a. Garden Burnet and Common Burnet, this plant's name is drawn from its brownish flowers.

hence it often became equated with obsessive crushes.

It garners only a single mention, in *Henry V*, an element in the Duke of Burgundy's ecological screed, but Francis Bacon echoes its sweetness, recommending it to line pathways, alongside wild THYME and MINT, for its sensorial delights.

C

CABBAGE – Variously known as cole, worts, and coleworts [among other names], Cabbage plays perfectly into the lingual salad Falstaff makes of the Latin and English that Parson Evans speaks in his thick Welsh accent. Cabbage was a staple food of cottage gardens and pottage for the impoverished; Gerard also highlights medicinal uses for poor eyesight, and notes that the seeds can fade freckles.

CANKER-BLOOM / CANKER-BLOSSOM – Not a flower per se, but mentioned enough that it warrants an entry: A canker is an open wound, often due to injury, that becomes infected with bacteria or creeping fungus that makes it fester, corrode, and ultimately die. Shakespeare made much of the phenomenon metaphorically, on plants and flowers, sometimes to comic but mostly tragic effect.

CAMOMILE [*var.* CHAMO-MILE] – A groundcover in the sixteenth century and a soothing aromatic herb—fifth of the nine magic herbs cited in the *Lacnunga,* a tenth-century Anglo-Saxon herbal—it symbolized energy, as well as humility because it grows stronger, faster, and more fragrant the more it is walked all over.

CAPER – A bramble-like shrub whose flower buds are pickled for

use as seasoning or garnish. Sir Toby puns on its use as sauce for the mutton, but a caper is also a dance derived from the late-sixteenth-century French *capriole*—the word *caper* echoes the name of a maneuver in classical riding, where the horse leaps from the ground kicking out with its hind legs. Hence, it is the basis for wordplay between Sir Toby and Andrew Aguecheek.

CARAWAY, CARRAWAYS / CARROWAYES – Mistakenly called seeds, these tiny fruits are related to FENNEL; they were made into comfits [a sort of candy; *see* SUGAR], helped mask the smell of rotting teeth, and were prescribed as accompaniments to APPLES. In his 1584 *Haven of Health,* Thomas Cogan helpfully notes that "all such things as breed wind, would be eaten with other things that breake wind." Their soft leathery shells, and the context of the line, indicate that they are in fact the "leather-coats" referenced, as opposed to a type of apple.

CARDUUS BENEDICTUS / HOLY THISTLE – In the *Poore Man's Jewell* of 1578, Thomas Brasbridge extolls the virtues of Carduus Benedictus as a curative "hearbe." Also known as Holy [or blessed] Thistle, its use to Shakespeare was through teasing wordplay with Beatrice, that the

remedy for her "qualm" contained the name of its cause, her romantic sparring partner, Benedick.

CARNATIONS / GILLY-VORS / PINKS – Carnation is twice mentioned by Shakespeare as a color [a light or deep rose-pink], hated by Falstaff and desired by Costard in a ribbon [it was an "in" color at court; Queen Elizabeth was gifted carnation-colored clothing over one hundred times during her reign]. As a flower, Carnation is paired up with Gillyvors [a.k.a. Juillet [July] flowers] in Perdita's speech against them as "Nature's bastards." In a conversation fraught with metaphor, her future father-in-law argues for the hybridization of Nature and Art through grafting, although botanic splicing of this kind was considered blasphemous, against Nature and God's plan. Both belong to the family of Pinks, which itself is punned on in a bawdy exchange between Romeo and Mercutio.

CARROT [*var.* CARET] – A root vegetable staple among commoners, and as such the root of the pun made by Mistress Quickly when Parson Evans, in his heavy Welsh accent, gives William a "caret" in his Latin lesson. Gerard delineates medicinal and culinary uses for yellow and red garden carrots, as well as for the whiter wild carrots.

CEDAR – An evergreen conifer of majestic reputation, it is several times used as a symbol of ancient lineage, or emblematically, via biblical descriptions of its height, strength, and longevity.

CHERRY – A poetic staple beginning with its rich red color, usually pertaining to lips. The growth pattern of the fruit doubled on a single stem offers a metaphor for closeness, or similarity. Cherries were popular with Henry VIII, and had a long association with virginity—a ballad involving Cherries and the Virgin Mother harks back to medieval times—making it an acceptable motif in the Virgin Queen's wardrobe. But the game of Cherry-pit [cherry stones tossed into a little hole, like a marble toss] is referred to in terms of the Devil.

CHESTNUT – Like the WALNUT, the luxuriant Chestnut tree has been soaring and spreading its branches in England for centuries. The sweet nuts were a dessert, or were preserved in the larder for lean months. Roasting was popular, with the attendant loud pop Petruchio notes. Their reddish brown hue establishes Orlando's hair color.

CLOVER – Delicate and sweetly scented, it was encouraged on sandy ground and grassy meadows for sheep and cattle to graze upon. Previously it was assumed that HONEY-STALKS also referred to clover, but recent research has shown that that notion originated in the eighteenth century without basis.

CLOVE – Unopened flower buds of the Clove tree, an evergreen and ancient trading staple from the East Indies. Both medicinal and culinary [apple pies were rarely made without them]; stuck into citrus fruits to make pomanders.

COCKLE – A flowering weed in the grass family, Corn Cockle has a delicate attractiveness that belies its toxicity. Much like DARNEL, its presence in harvest crops meant labor-intensive hand weeding to remove it. Metaphorically, its presence suggests corruption of some nature, which is why [despite the fact that it is also a shell], it shows up in the ravings of the mad girls, Ophelia, and the Jailer's Daughter.

COLOQUINTIDA – Nicknamed bitter apple, but actually a type of GOURD originally cultivated in Cyprus or Spain, so an apt fruit for Iago to reference. Writers contemporary with Shakespeare, such as John Lyly and Robert Greene, noted its acrid and poisonous nature; Gerard cautions that medicinally it is a forceful purgative.

COLUMBINE – This garden and wild flower could have been called *Aquilegia*, because the petals suggest eagle talons; others see doves in flight [Latin: *Columba*]; or it could have been called *Chelidonia* [celandine] "for it bloometh in the coming of sparrows" and was believed to restore their eyesight. An interesting claim, given Hamlet's "fall of a sparrow" speech in the last act of the play. The curved, hornlike spikes at the ends of the five petals connect Columbine to cuckoldry; the layers of meaning when Ophelia doles it out during her "mad scene" have been rife with interpretation. As a heraldic emblem, it was a feature of both the House of Lancaster and the Derby family. But springing as it does from the Ranunculus family, and so related to ACONITUM, it is poisonous.

CORK – Gerard gives a thorough description of the Mediterranean tree in his *Herball*. The thick, spongy, lightweight bark was ideal for women's shoes, as heels and lining for warmth, so prized that it appears in the Gift Rolls for Queen Elizabeth. But its ubiquity, then as now, is as bottle stoppers.

CORN – A generic term for grain, especially a lead crop, or any crop that requires grinding, be it WHEAT, RYE, OATS, or BARLEY—the many mentions in Shakespeare have caused modern audiences some confusion. Turkie Corne, a.k.a. maize, was introduced to England in the sixteenth century—Gerard displays it on the cover of his 1597 *Herball*, in the left hand of the mysterious "Fourth Man." His in-depth coverage traces its roots and routes from Turkey [hence its name], Asia, and America, perhaps compounding confusion in calling it Turkie Wheate. He also explains his experience of growing it, though it wasn't cultivated as a crop for consumption until the late seventeenth century. The price and availability of "corn" was key to the stability of the kingdom. Corn rebellions broke out in the 1590s [echoed in *Henry VI* and *Coriolanus*], prompting Burghley, the Queen's Lord Treasurer in 1597, to address Parliament about "the lamentable cry of the poor who are likely to perish by . . . the dearness and high price of corn."

COWSLIP – A close relative of the OXSLIP and the PRIMROSE, this native spring flower is distinguished by its "freckles," five tiny red dots at its center, enough to hang a plot point on [*Cymbeline*]. Shakespeare makes the bell of the flower, nicknamed Fairy Cups, a nesting nook; the "rubies" claim to be key to a clear complexion. Describing the flowers as Tatiana's "tall pensioners" isn't entirely fanciful: Queen Elizabeth's Gentlemen Pensioners were always the "tallest and goodliest gentlemen and Yeomen the Kingdom." Cowslips feature among the embroidered flowers on the iconic Rainbow Portrait of Elizabeth.

CRAB-APPLE – Grandfather to subsequent cultivated APPLE trees; this native tree acted as stock onto which new Apple varieties could be grafted. Populous in Shakespeare, often as just CRABS, they are synonymous with sourness, much like we would describe a "crabby" person today. The fruit is hard and ill-formed, so roasting was necessary for eating; mashing was an option, too, from which was made verjuice, a sort of vinegar used for cooking, preserving, and as a medicament. Among the sacred herbs of the Anglo-Saxon *Lacnunga*, the wood of the Wilding tree [Gerard's name for it] was particularly sturdy, thus desirable for walking sticks and staves.

CROW-FLOWERS – In Gertrude's specific list of Ophelia's

garland flowers, this one has been something of a mystery, but Gerard identifies it as the Ragged-Robin, a delicate wetland flower.

CROWN IMPERIAL – The sole mention of this second Fritillary [the first being the ADONIS FLOWER], new to England c. 1580 via Constantinople, comes in the pastoral scenes of *Winter's Tale*. In 1595, playwright George Chapman called it "Fair Crown Imperial, Emperor of Flowers" in Ovid's *Banquet of Sense*. Its large golden blooms form a circlet at the top of the plant like a crown, with green tufts sprouting from the center, but legend holds that though it was admired in the garden of Gethsemane, on the last night, when Jesus was taken away, all the flowers bowed their heads in sorrow *except* the Crown Imperial. Subsequently doomed to droop its head in perpetuity, it even emanates a tear-like substance. Gerard, who seems unaware of its kinship to the Adonis Flower [*Fritillaria meleagris*], also put the Crown Imperial on the cover of his great *Herball*.

CUCKOO-BUDS – A variety of buttercup native to England.

CUCKOO-FLOWERS – *see* LADY-SMOCKS.

CURRANTS – English currants, akin to GOOSE-

BERRIES, grow wild across much of Britain. They don't seem to have been domesticated until the sixteenth century; Gerard mentions them in London gardens as a small fruit "without prickes . . . of a perfect red colour," as in *Two Noble Kinsmen*. But on the Clown's shopping list they are, Reverend Ellacombe insists, the Currants of commerce, *Vitis Corinthiaca*— from Corinth; in the thirteenth and fourteenth centuries, they were called *raisins de Corauntz*.

CUPID'S FLOWER – *see* PANSY.

CYME/SENNA – The First Folio has Cyme; later amended to Senna, the assumption was that it was a misprint of "cynne," an archaic spelling of *senna*. While Senna per se was not introduced until the mid-seventeenth century, its use as a purgative is documented back to preclassical times.

CYPRESS – An evergreen import from Italy or the Mediterranean, notably Cyprus, dark and pencil-thin. Its preservative qualities make it an ideal wood for storage chests. Strewn in times of plague, Cypress became part of mourning rituals. It indicated a range of emotions around death, from sadness to sanctity.

D

DAFFODIL/NARCISSUS – A wild woodland flower brought in to brighten knot gardens, these early bloomers were happy harbingers of the approaching spring. But the connection with the Greek

myth of Narcissus meant the flower could also signify foolishness.

DAISIES – Native to Britain, the common Daisy is herald to spring and summer. Daisies were

symbolic of freshness, innocence, and modesty, but also, because each flower is short-lived, they stood for grief, sadness, and death.

DAMSON – *see* PLUM.

DARNEL – A grain grass or weed commonly found in harvest fields, and highly toxic. If the seeds invaded baking or brewing grains, the results were dangerous, producing a delirium akin to drunkenness, and blurred vision. Another irritant was the cost and time required to remove the seedlings by hand. *See* COCKLE.

DATES – The exotic fruit of the Date Palm [found throughout Southern Europe, North Africa, and Western Asia]. Dates were coveted imports harking back centuries; the Anglo-Saxons called them Finger-Apples.

DEAD MEN'S FINGERS – *see* LONG PURPLES.

DEWBERRIES – Ripening earlier than Blackberries, they have larger, but fewer drupes [the bulbous clusters that compose the juicy berry]; the trailing bush never grows as large as the BLACK-BERRY. *See also* BILBERRY.

DIAN'S BUD – *see* WORMWOOD.

DOCKS – Broad-leaved, deep-rooted weeds that favor neglected pasture and meadow, they often grow near stinging NETTLES, which is convenient given that they are a soothing antidote for the burning sensation.

E

EBONY – For Shakespeare, this hardwood tree is just a stand-in for the intense color in the heart of its trunk, a jet-black wood that takes a high polish. Ebony was briefly considered a candidate for HEBENON/HEBONA.

EGLANTINE – a.k.a. Sweet Brier, the wild rose with a slight prickle was cherished for its singular sweet scent, deemed superior to that of any other Rose; it emanates from the leaves, not the bloom, and can't be duplicated [hence you'll never find a true Eglantine perfume]. Perhaps that is why Queen Elizabeth adopted it as a personal emblem, alongside the more formal Tudor Rose.

ELDER – The native tree is a familiar in woods and on rough ground, its honey-scented flowers in stark contrast to its stinking leaves. Shakespeare makes use, via pun, of the legend that Judas hung himself on this tree, and that its stems are used by small boys to make popguns. Elder is renowned as "nature's medicine chest," which is why the Host includes it among Aescalapius and Galen in addressing Dr. Caius.

ELM – Beautifully ornamental and prized for their timber, Elms are basically now extinct in England due to disease [although there are attempts to revive them]; Romans planted them in vineyards and Ovid echoed the ancients in noting the love between the Elm and VINE.

ERINGOES – a.k.a. Sea Holly, it was cultivated as a vegetable with various medicinal uses. Shakespeare is first to mention it, in Falstaff's famous line that aligns the candied root with two other popular aphrodisiacs, sweet potatoes and musk-flavored sugar candy called kissing-comfits.

F

FENNEL – A hardy perennial herb whose heady scent of aniseed hinted at its digestive uses. Chewing Fennel seeds helped stave off hunger, and it was appreciated as a carminative in a staple diet of beans and pulses. Although revered as one of the nine sacred herbs, Gerard didn't even bother including Fennel in his *Herball;* it was so well known, he considered it "lost labor" to write about.

FERN/FERN SEED – The joke in Shakespeare's dialogue is that "Fern-seed" is invisible [the "seeds" are actually tiny spores] so, invoking the Doctrine of Signatures, meaning like to like, it could theoretically reproduce invisibility, but only on Midsummer Eve. Good thing there was a caveat.

FESCUE – A large genus of native Grasses, possibly utilized for schoolroom instruction [an anonymous 1607 play, *The Puritan,* uses the plant in a similar fashion], although in *Two Noble Kinsmen* there are sexual undertones as well. *See* GRASSES.

FIG – Medicinal applications aside, the Fig's sexually suggestive shape and renown as an aphrodisiac gave rise to much bawdy humor. Reverend Ellacombe beautifully illuminates an extraordinary aspect of the Fig: that it is "neither fruit nor flower, [but] partaking of both, … the fleshy receptacle enclosing a multitude of flowers which never see the light, yet come to full perfection and ripen their seed." Given his calling as a canon of the Church, however, he sidestepped clarifying the meaning of Pistol's exchanges, particularly the crude gesture of "making a fig"—putting the thumb between the first two fingers—roughly, the "female" version of "flipping a bird." Or flicking the thumb out from the mouth or teeth. Accompanying this gesture with the Spanish word for fig further underscored the emphatic nature of the epithet, since the gesture itself was thought to have originated in Spain.

FILBERT – see HAZEL.

FLAGS – Candidates include the native yellow Iris, common in wetlands; the term could also embrace any floating REED or RUSH. See also FLOWER-DE-LUCE.

FLAX – A cultivated crop pre-dating the Dark Ages, it is spun into sailcloth, cordage, and linen, and is the origin of linseed oil. Exceedingly flammable; its pale fibers have also been compared to hair in old age. Given that its Latin name is *Linum usitatissimum* and that it was spun into line or linen, it seems a fair candidate for the "Line-grove" mentioned in *Tempest*. See LINE TREE [LIME/LINDEN].

FLOWER-DE-LUCE/ FLEUR-DE-LIS – Various lilies and irises have been posited for this flower, which is, as the Fleur-de-lis, the cognizance of France. The French *lys* does mean lily, but irises have long been symbols of royalty; Edmund Spenser, Francis Bacon,

and Ben Jonson all write of the Flower-de-luce as an Iris. Representative of faith, valor, and wisdom, the emblem arguably stands on its own as a heraldic symbol, apart from identification with any particular plant.

FUMITER/FUMITORY/ FENITAR – Handsome but undesirable, these weeds can eat up a grain field.

FURROW-WEEDS – Any plants that grow in the furrowed ground left by the plow; see COCKLE, DARNEL, FUMITER, GRASSES.

FURZE/GOSS/GORSE – Gorse is the standard appellation for Shakespeare's Furze and Goss that populate Prospero's wild island. For these dense, sharp, spreading shrubs that proliferate on acidic soil and heathland, the operative element here is their rough and wild aspect. See THORNS, BROOM, BRIER.

G

GARLIC/GARLICKE – Renowned for cleaning the blood, preventing colds, and adding a rich flavor to meats, soups, and stews, it is a pungent member of the ONION family, and was often associated with the poor or immigrants. It has particular associations with witchcraft, but is more notorious for its strong smell, causing bad breath and body odor, hence Bottom's caution to the actors.

GILLIVORS/GILLY-FLOWERS – Clove-scented blooms in the PINK family. See CARNATIONS.

GINGER – Familiar but not native, the perennial tuberous root was a common import from the East Indies; its reputation for "hotting up" food and drink made it a valuable commodity for bringing flavor to a bland diet. Popular as a medicinal and for making gingerbread.

GOOSEBERRY – In the CURRANT family, this garden shrub was cultivated for its larger, sweeter fruit. The green berries have nothing to do with geese so when Shakespeare references the fruit in a shortened moniker, i.e., "goose," it can cause confusion, es-

pecially when he's just referencing the color. But because Shakespeare is sneaky with his layered meanings, "goose" can mean the green berry, the fowl, and a prostitute in a single mention. "Gooseberry" itself is an Anglicized version of its French or Italian name, or a corruption of *Crossberry*. The fruit was recommended during times of plague, and is probably at the root of the idiom "silly goose," harking from May Day festivals.

GOURD/PUMPION/ MARROW/CURBITA – Various edible Gourds of the

Cucurbit family. *Pumpion* was often used generically for any edible gourd including melons and cucumbers, hence Mistress Ford's "gross watery . . ." description. Marrow, too, in *Timon*, is in this family. Too tempting to exclude: Parolles' line about "curbed time"—as Curbita, its context perfectly plays on the family name. Pistol's gourd is actually a kind of dice, possibly made from the dried outer casing of a small gourd.

GRAPES, RAISINS [*see also* **VINE**] – The fruit of the vine, *Grapes* could be a synonym for

the wine they become, an alternative name for berry, or a generic reference to fruit. As the dried fruits, Raisins, also called muscatels, are a corruption of *racemus*, meaning a bunch of Grapes [which happens to be the tavern name in *Measure for Measure*], and so could just mean the ripe clusters still hanging on the tree.

GRASSES/STOVER/ HONEY-STALKS – General herbage in pastures or meadows; botanically, any number of over ten thousand varieties within the family Poaceae—they

grow quickly and bounce back easily from excessive foot traffic. Thus, Grasses can symbolize strength, self-sufficiency, and regeneration. Shakespeare employs them in myriad ways, from the callous imagery of mowing down women and children to the gently poetic headrest. Groundcover—another option, can be seen at **MUSH-ROOMS/TOADSTOOLS**. We umbrella Honey-stalks in here as fodder [*see* **CLOVER**] due to the recent research showing that the term probably just refers to dewy Grasses favored by sheep. *See also* **FESCUE**.

H

HAREBELL – It is hotly debated whether Shakespeare meant Harebell; Bluebell, which blooms with the Primrose; or Wild Hyacinth, whose vernacular name was Harebell [and which *does* have veins]. We chose what he wrote because, as noted [*see* **PEONY**], Shakespeare usually knows best.

HAWTHORN/MAY TREE – Beloved herald of the spring, its mayflowers blooming in time for May Day fairs, and as shelter for shepherds, the tree was associated with country folk. Nicknames include Whitethorn, Blackthorn, and Quickthorn for its abundant spikes, sometimes used as a rustic acupuncture; also fairy tree for its magical powers. Its ripe red berries, called Cuckoo's Beads or Pixie Cups, could make a cardiac tonic.

HAZEL/FILBERT/ FILBERD/PHILBIRTES and **NUTS** – This multiuse shrub served as hedgerow, wattle

fence, and nut farm. Its flexible, coppiced stems, used for water dowsing, were responsible for its magical reputation, apparent in Mercutio's Queen Mab speech. When Shakespeare uses the term *nut*, it is assumed he means Filbert, the name for the cultivated nut, derived from its apparently very specific ripening time: August 22, St. Philbert's Day. *See also* **ALMOND, CHEST-NUT, WALNUT.**

HEATH – Open moorland covered with a variety of native flowering shrubbery and Grasses, or the growth itself, called Heath, or Heather, Bell Heather, and Ling [the last sometimes replacing "long" in *Tempest*, although "long" is likely the correct reading]. So admired was this wild growth that cultivated gardens were intentionally fashioned to mimic the naturally occurring landscape.

HEBENON/HEBONA – The poison that killed Hamlet's

father continues to be a hot topic in that everyone is seduced into trying to solve the mystery of what exact toxin is poured in his ear. We are no exceptions and have reasoned out a solution, but also offer a composite of poisons for your consideration.

– Hebenon is the name of the poison in the First Folio; Hebona comes from the two Quartos of *Hamlet*. But none of the source material for the story names any specific poison at all—it seems to be solely Shakespeare's addition.

– In his play *The Jew of Malta*, Christopher Marlowe cites "juice of hebon" as a deadly poison.

– Edmund Spenser, who styled himself an antique poet, employs the arcane term in *Fairie Queene*: "trees of bitter gall and Heben sad," and the wood is carved into a "deadly Heben bow," a "speare of Heben wood," and a "Heben launce."

- John Gower, a fourteenth-century poet whose work is an acknowledged Shakespeare source, writes "Of Hebenus that sleepy tree," and later, "She his sleepy ears pierceth" in his poem *Confessio Amantis.*

So those are the several mentions of a poisonous source by major influences on Shakespeare for his "Hebenon" in *Hamlet.* The possibilities for what Hebenon actually is:

- INSANE ROOT – In *Macbeth,* and identified by scholars as Henbane; Gerard actually calls it Insana. But *Henbane* as an echo of *Hebona* is not strong enough to make it the leading candidate. Plus, its effects are different than what the Ghost describes.

- EBONY – Or *ebon,* is another homophone, but the Ebony tree was an expensive import, not easily available, and distilling from its resin was too difficult; plus, it's negligible as a poison.

- HEMLOCK – Works faster if taken in wine [a distillation], but again, its effects as a poison don't match.

- ACONITE – This poison isn't even considered a candidate, presumably because the effects don't coincide with the Ghost's.

But neither do they with Romeo's death, even though it is posited as his poison. In a low dose, it numbs all the limbs, as in a coma, so it would fit with what the Friar gives Juliet to fake her death, however.

- DEADLY NIGHT-SHADE – Called *enoron* in Old English [a slight echo of *Hebenon*], but Belladonna now; it is known for its toxicity and availability, but symptoms include dizziness, delirium, and convulsions.

- YEW – Being a tree, it fits perfectly with the earlier cited old-fashioned mentions of Heben, and its toxic effects are in sync with the Ghost's symptoms, including a crusting of the skin, and mimicking a snakebite. Plus, tellingly, Hamlet's father would have used an antique term.

HEMLOCK – In the benign family of CARROT, FEN-NEL, and Cow PARSLEY. HEMLOCK's reputation as a poison precedes it thanks to Socrates' suicide story; a jot can serve as a sedative, or antidote, but just a wee bit over can result in paralysis or death. Given poison's association with the Black Arts, it is not surprising that one of the *Macbeth* Witches uses it, referring to the superstition

that it is more potent when dug up at night. *See* HEBENON / HEBONA, KECKSIES.

HEMP – A cultivated crop in increasing demand in the island maritime nation: its fiber was made into canvas, cordage [including the hangman's noose], and coarse fabric.

HERB OF GRACE [*also* GRACE] – *see* RUE.

HOLLY – A slow-growing evergreen with attractive red berries but sharp, repelling leaves. Male and female flowers are borne on separate trees, so they need to be planted in groups to thrive.

HOLY THISTLE – *see* CARDUUS BENEDICTUS.

HONEY-STALKS – *see* CLOVER and GRASSES.

HONEYSUCKLE / WOODBINE – Native climber with an intensely sensual scent; Woodbine had been considered a more generic creeper, but the plants slowly became entwined much like their growth pattern, which, coupled with the heady fragrance, made them symbolic of ardent and steadfast love.

HYSSOP – An aromatic evergreen herb, bitter to the taste. It was often planted with THYME as they were thought to stimulate each other's growth, but Iago pulls one up in favor of the other.

I

INSANE ROOT – Mentioned by Banquo in *Macbeth* as if to say, "Are we crazy?" It is identified as Henbane, a poison

that the Roman natural philosopher Pliny called "offensive to the understanding"; it could produce a maniacal delirium but was also

used as a "dangerous sedative for the insane." *See* HEBENON / HEBONA.

IVY - A native climbing plant, it was considered feminine because of its twining habit. Its evergreen leaves signify immortality, but Shakespeare also draws human parallels in its unchecked growth and smothering habits.

K

KECKSIES - A low, hairy herb with a creeping stem, but the solitary flowers, like wee snapdragons, are rather handsome. Thomas and Faircloth note in their excellent dictionary, "Its only appearance [in *Henry V*] is in a catalogue of weeds which paints a woeful picture of the French landscape following the English invasion." Previously posited as a colloquialism for HEMLOCK, *Kickxia spuria* has the distinction of the common name of round-leaved fluellin, Fluellen being a character in the play who rather fits its description.

KNOT-GRASS - Not a grass, just a jointed weed with a creeping habit. It strangles other plants in its path and is tough to eradicate; assumed to stunt growth if sipped as an infusion.

L

LADY-SMOCKS/ CUCKOO-FLOWERS - Meadow flowers perhaps named for clothes strewn in the fields to dry [a common custom over LAVEN-DER fields]. Its alternate moniker may reflect the return of the cuckoo; it was noted for flowering round about Lady Day, March 25, also known as New Year's Day for Elizabethans, when the calendar year number changed.

LARK'S-HEELS - This flower, thought to be Larkspur, makes a solo appearance, in the flower-filled song in *Two Noble Kinsmen*.

LAVENDER - A favorite of the knot gardens so popular in Queen Elizabeth's time for their formal geometric designs and opportunity to show off exotic imports in neat hedges; also a strewing herb to banish bad smells, freshen laundry by laying linen out on swathes of it, and as a scented sedative. Perdita calls it "hot Lavender" because it thrives in high heat.

LEATHER-COAT - *See* APPLE and CARAWAY.

LEEK - In the Onion family, a staple food of the poor because it's easy to grow. Shakespeare mines it for comic effect for its color and Welsh connections—it is the national emblem of Wales.

LEMON - Popular in cooking and perfumes; lined with CLOVES, LEMONS stepped in for ORANGES as pomanders. Also provided opportunities for wordplay, interchanged with *leman* as *lover*.

LETTUCE - In every herb garden for "salad days," often used generically for various greens used for salads. Lettuce could stimulate the appetite, aid digestion, sooth a hangover, and double as both aphrodisiac and anaphrodisiac—quite a feat.

LILY/LILY OF THE VALLEY - The Madonna Lily has long been the poetic barometer of whiteness, clear skin, delicate fingers, virginity . . . and lily-livered. But Lily of the Valley, too, is a candidate for some of these comparisons, still white, but a better fit for "small as a wand."

LINE TREE [LIME/ LINDEN] - This threefold mention happens in *Tempest,* and it seems to be the Line-grove line that prompted the identification as the fragrant Lime or Linden tree. But given that Lime/Linden trees are unlikely to call a [Mediterranean] island climate home, that the other two references are clearly to laundry, and that Line is also a term for FLAX [derived from the Latin], the wrong tree may have been barked up all these years.

LOCUST/CAROB TREE - Locust beans, fruit of the exotic Carob tree, were used as a sweetener; a precursor for chocolate, which Elizabethans would never taste [it didn't debut in England till the 1650s]. Native to the Mediterranean, especially Spain and

Cyprus—remarkably site-specific for Iago's diabolical observation.

LONG PURPLES/DEAD MEN'S FINGERS – A debated bloom in the long list of plants Gertrude recites in her report of Ophelia's death, but her further description: "that liberal shepherds give a grosser name" clinches it for the Cuckoo-pint [a.k.a. lords-and-ladies, wild arum] since it perfectly fulfills all the specifications: it's long, it's purple, it could look like a dead finger, or a naughtier body part. Even Dr. Levi Fox of the Shakespeare Birthplace Trust forwent the previous ID of "early purple orchid" in favor of the flower that more "aptly conveys" the poet's meaning.

M

MACE – see NUTMEG.

MALLOW – The common, or wild Mallow, originally a wasteland denizen, can also be cultivated. Its solo mention is in the context of its intrusive nature as a weed.

MANDRAGORA / MANDRAKE – The forked root of this poisonous, narcotic plant is often anthropomorphized into screaming men or shrieking creatures dug out of the earth. Probably a sixteenth-century introduction, but Mandrake was in regular use much earlier. Although the terms were interchangeable, *mandrake* is usually the plant; *mandragora* is the drug. Mandrake had myriad health benefits, but when administered with poppy, it had a particular potency.

MARIGOLD/MARY-BUD – Mary-buds is the name Cloten in *Cymbeline* uses for Marigolds, whose flowers have the charming habit of following the sun to open and close; Marigold is sometimes borrowed for other plants with similar behavior. It was used for hair color and also as a cheap substitute for SAFFRON to color and flavor food. Figurative associations included death, resurrection, and hope.

MARJORAM – A staple culinary and strewing herb, the native plant, especially the sweet version, had a host of medicinal applications: to comfort the brain, for melancholy, urinary retention, and, usefully, as an antidote to poison. Its scent made it popular bound up in fragrant posies to inhale as an antidote to the stench of sixteenth-century hygiene.

MARROW – see GOURD/PUMPION.

MAST – see ACORN.

MEDLAR – A fruit fraught with metaphor in Shakespeare, beyond the wordplay with *medlar/meddler*. The small russet "apple" is inedible until it has begun to rot, a fact Shakespeare mines for sexual innuendo. Scholars have glossed the fruit as female genitalia to explain the scenes where it appears, but recent commentators have cried foul. The fruit in French is called *cul de chien* [dog's arse tree], in English slang, the "open-arse" fruit, so it's pretty clear where Mercutio is suggesting that Romeo put his "Poperin' pear." Once you've got that, the scenes where Medlar is mentioned become clear. Or clear*er*. It helps to see the fruit.

MINT – Kitchen and strewing herb, a staple for cooks and medical practitioners who could determine which of a wide variety would serve their purpose. Mints have a laundry list of medicinal applications.

MISTLETOE – Evergreen and parasitic, Mistletoe appears near the tops of an array of trees such as APPLE, OAK, Poplar, and LIME. Beloved by Druids for its magical protection, the Scandinavians believed that the god of Peace was killed by an arrow of Mistletoe, and when his life was restored it was moved to the protection of the goddess of Love; kissing underneath a sliver of it honors its transformation from a missive of destruction into one of love.

MOSS – True Mosses grow in large quantities in damp places, on stones or trees; Moss could fill or line roofs, and was collected as bedding for cattle. Moss could signify age, venerability, wildness, and lack of civilized discourse … or the grave.

MULBERRIES – Both the White and the Black Mulberry are in the same botanical family as the FIG. Whereas the white is a fast-growing tree, the black, dedicated by the Ancients to Minerva, is notably slow, with fruit so tender to the touch, the slightest pressure causes stain. In the source story from Ovid's *Metamorphoses*, the fruit was originally white, so the tree Thisbe finds shade under is likely the White Mulberry. In 1609, King

James had a get-rich-quick scheme: To be a player in the growing silk trade, he bought 100,000 mulberry trees and set his worms to work. The problem? His were Black; silkworms only eat White Mulberry leaves.

MUSHROOM / TOAD-STOOL – Fleshy fungal orbs, Mushrooms generally represent the edible species, while Toadstools are the toxic ones. Both home and dance floor for fairy rings, Mushrooms are renowned for their rapid growth.

MUSTARD – In the CAB-BAGE family, mustard includes the native black Mustard but can refer to any plant of the family, and almost any of them can be made into the condiment; Tewksbury indicates where it was made. Mustard plasters were conventional poultices. The biblical quote about having the faith of a Mustard seed refers to how tiny they are, an indication of the size of Titania's fairy minion, Mustardseed.

MYRTLE – A small evergreen tree with dark, shiny leaves, soft wood, and creamy, aromatic flowers. Traditional in wedding garlands, wreaths, and bouquets, perhaps because Venus was honored with the planting of myrtle groves.

N

NARCISSUS – *see* DAFFODIL.

NETTLES – Populating open pasture, stinging Nettles cause considerable discomfort, a burning sensation [although they are revered as number six of the nine sacred herbs]. *Nettle* in general can refer to any plant with similar irritating qualities, lending itself easily to metaphor. Comforting caveat: The remedy is always nearby, in the form of DOCK leaves.

NUTMEG / MACE – Native to the East Indies, the hard aromatic seed and the reddish aril [known as Mace], which is the covering to the kernel, were both coveted spices, valued for their herbal and medicinal benefits as well as for adding depth of flavor to foods.

O

OAK – Renowned for its size, long life, and fine wood, the Oak is replete with metaphor: strength, reliability, durability, solidity, toughness . . . Oak wreaths heralded victory; with their ACORNS, Oaks represented an investment in the future. Sometimes called Jove's tree due to its mighty reputation. There is a Duke's Oak [*A Midsummer Night's Dream*] in Sabbioneta, Italy, known as the Little Athens of the Renaissance thanks to the Gonzaga family. Herne's Oak in *Merry Wives of Windsor* is derived from the legend of Herne the Hunter, who reputedly lived in the time of Richard II.

OATS – A cereal grain grown for food and fodder, Oats were easier to grow, so cheaper and less valued than WHEAT. *Oaten* [like *Hempen*] was a derogatory term suggesting rustics rather than city sophisticates; oat straw provided reeds for rustic pipes.

OLIVE – From Greek mythological times, the Olive was an emblem of peace. And although it didn't proliferate as a tree in England, its fruits and oil were used and enjoyed.

ONION – In the genus with LEEK and GARLIC; all were eaten both raw and cooked, and generally associated with poorer folk. Onion's ability to cause bad breath and tears is older than Shakespeare.

ORANGE – The first of the citrus trees to be cultivated in England, by the late sixteenth century, Oranges were a ready commodity. Imported from Spain in large quantities, they were sold in theaters as refreshment, by "orange-women," who were considered little better than prostitutes [akin to coster-mongers, *see* APPLE].

OXLIP – Kissing cousins of COWSLIP and PRIMROSE, Oxlips are a deeper yellow, and their flowers fall all to one side; they rarely venture outside East Anglia.

P

PALM – Growing in tropical climes, the leaves or fronds were worn by pilgrims returning from the Holy Land or other religious sites. Branches were carried on Palm Sunday [WILLOW was often a local substitute]. From ancient times, the Palm symbolized peace and victory; it still implies preeminence or honor when expressed as "to bear the palm," "to yield the palm."

PANSY/LOVE-IN-IDLENESS – The native Heartsease, or wild Pansy was probably Shakespeare's Love-in-idleness. Its name was said to derive from the French *pensées*, meaning thoughts, as Ophelia says. Medicinal uses included the treatment of heart problems, hence the apt nickname.

PARMACETI – Shepherd's Purse a.k.a. Poor Man's Parmaceti, the juice of which, according to Gerard, could staunch internal bleeding, although the "inward bruise" Hotspur speaks of may not be a physical one. The Latin word *bursa*, meaning purse, could suggest a payoff was the best healer.

PARSLEY – A leafy kitchen garden staple and culinary herb, freshened meats, bulked up soups and stews.

PEACH – Skipping this fruit would have been justified since Shakespeare only mentions them in terms of color, but Elizabethans *were* acquainted with Peaches. The Queen was gifted at least seven times with boxes of the luscious fruit from Genoa. But she was far more often given peach-colored clothing: waistcoats, petticoats, nightgowns, sleeves [perhaps safer given that King John was said to have died from a surfeit of Peaches]. Fashion fads embraced the color of the year just as today's Pantone palette. Shakespeare references the color for satin and stockings, but also slips in the meaning to accuse [*im*peach].

PEAR/WARDEN – Just as available but more valued than the APPLE due to its sensitive flesh and, like the Apple, the fruit gives rise to metaphor—mostly sexual in nature [such as Parolles' comparison to the womb]. The Popering or, as Mercutio says when referencing the MEDLAR, "*Poperin'* pear," is the Flemish-named fruit used as a bawdy homophone for "pop her in." Warden [or Lukeward] Pears were considered good for baking.

PEAS/PEASE/PEASCOD/SQUASH – Fresh young Peas were a delicacy, but mostly the common kitchen-garden plant was fodder, or food for common folk. Peas were easily dried for winter and rehydrated [and preferable to the notoriously "windy" bean]. The pod or peas[e]cod contained the individual peas [and provided ample opportunities for sexual innuendo]; young peapods were called Squash. The fairy named Peaseblossom suggests a delicate, pretty little sprite.

PEONY – Over the years, various editors and scholars have mistaken "pioned" for "peony" [or "piony"] in the *Tempest* line "Thy banks with pioned and twilled brims . . ." Determined to sow flowers where there are none, the wishful thinking extended to changing "twilled" to "tulip'd" or "willow'd," even "lilied"! A more sober "fix" made it "tilled," better because *pion* is an archaic term for dig [and the root of *pioneer*], and *twilled* is defined as [variously], leveled, ridged, or trimmed, so those banks, like the other ground mentioned [leas, meads], are being prepared for plantings far less romantic than frilly flowers. In fact, *no* other flowers appear in the speech *or* scene. As happens so often, Shakespeare is usually right the first time. So you will find no peonies here.

PEPPER – Both the plant and its fruit were desirable commodities; the dried berries were cracked or ground with special boxes made to carry the spice, although "*peppercorn rent*" meant a nominal amount. *Peppered* meant to be pelted—the peppercorns perhaps recalling popguns—or ruined, done for.

PIG-NUT – Also called Earth-nuts, this native plant of grasslands and woodlands has sweetish, edible tuberous roots, but they leave a sour aftertaste. More commonly eaten in Shakespeare's day, but still popular with pigs, who will dig for them.

PIMPERNELL – The [scarlet] Pimpernell, first name Henry in the Induction scene of *Taming of the Shrew*, pops up alongside his buddy Peter Turph, as part closes up under threatening skies, and is pictured on page 6 since, as a Character, it has no quotes attributed to it.

PINE - General consensus points to the Scots Pine, a tall evergreen valued for its resin and long, straight trunks used as ships' masts. Figuratively, Shakespeare mines its comparative majesty, height, and strength.

PINKS - *see* CARNATIONS.

PIPPIN - *see* APPLE.

PLANE - The sole mention, in *Two Noble Kinsmen*, of this spreading tree with large leaves and smooth bark is not to be confused with the familiar "London" Plane, a circa seventeenth-century hybrid [but *plane did sometimes* refer to the SYCAMORE due to similarity of foliage].

PLANTAIN, PLANTAN - Shakespeare is not talking about a banana leaf; this common weed found by roadsides was one of the nine sacred Anglo-Saxon herbs, prized for its medicinal properties, especially as an astringent to treat wounds and staunch blood flow. It's essentially a Band-Aid, which is why Romeo uses it as gentle sarcasm in response to Benvolio's lame romantic advice. It's a part of

Moth's joke in *Love's Labour's Lost* when he questions how an APPLE [Costard] could have a shin wound. The "plantage" Troilus refers to is more likely a reference to plants in general.

PLUMS / PLUM TREE / DAMSONS / PRUNES - Succulent fruits found wild and in orchards, favorites in pottage or puddings; gum from the bark had medicinal uses, as did Prunes, the dried fruit preserved to overwinter, or stewed to soften, and serving as a laxative. Damsons are plum-like fruits too tart to eat raw so made into conserves, but they also had sexual connotations. *Prunes,* sometimes associated with brothels, declined in popularity in the sixteenth century in favor of *Raisins,* although the terms were often interchangeable.

POMEGRANATE - The small fruit-bearing tree was widely cultivated in warm countries. Symbolic of sexuality and fertility because of its abundance of kernels but, as the emblem of Persephone, queen of the underworld, its mention by Juliet is foreboding. At one time thought to be the apple of Eden. A more peculiar mention in *Henry IV* suggests it is the name of a room in the tavern.

POMEWATER - *see* APPLE.

POPERING - *see* PEAR.

POPPY - Iago is invoking the Opium Poppy, renowned for its narcotic and soporific properties. Even more menacingly, the flower had serious to fatal side effects if used together with Mandrake.

POTATO - You say Potato, they say Sweet Potato ... Scholars debate which tuber is meant, although the Sweet Potato, considered an aphrodisiac ["procuring bodily lust," said Gerard], fits for Falstaff's line [*see* ERINGOES], and it certainly looks more like a finger for Thersites' insult. But Gerard is also pictured proudly holding the new "Virginia" potatoes, which he called bastards.

PRIMROSE - Sort of the primary sibling in a family that includes COWSLIPS and OXLIPS, this plant's pretty yellow flowers, almost always described as pale, pop up on banks and leas in early spring, so can represent the first or best of something [first flowering, first fruits]. Following the *primrose path* suggests blithely taking a course of action without foresight or proper consideration.

PRUNES - *see* PLUMS.

PUMPION - *see* GOURD / MARROW.

Q

QUINCE - Akin to the PEAR, but too hard and tart to eat raw, Quince is cooked into pies [a popular gift for Queen Elizabeth], jellies, and marmalades; its

reputation for increasing fertility and fostering smarter children made it a must for pregnant women and brides, hence its inclusion in Juliet's marriage preparations.

And Peter Quince, the carpenter of *A Midsummer Night's Dream*? Perhaps he has a tart personality.

R

RADISH ‒ Fodder for food, and Falstaff's fantasies, Radishes could be eaten cooked or raw, or carved as Imogen does [*see* TURNIP]; used medically they reputedly made one thin and could cure baldness.

RAISINS ‒ *see* GRAPES.

REEDS ‒ Shakespeare uses these plants, found en masse at water's edge or in marshlands, more often descriptively than purposely, as for thatch. As hair, a thin voice, a metaphor for fright or weakness, Reeds were ubiquitous, utilitarian, and humble according to Aesop's fable of the OAK and the Reed. *See* RUSHES, GRASSES.

RHUBARB ‒ The sole mention in *Macbeth* attests to the fact that Rhubarb was used medicinally, rather than eaten in Shakespeare's time. Gerard illustrates Turkie, or Turkish Rhubarb, as do we.

RICE ‒ The only mention of this imported grain is the shopping list in *Winter's Tale*. Reverend Ellacombe suggests Shakespeare may have seen the plant growing in Gerard's London garden.

ROSE ‒ Is defining a Rose possible? Perhaps it is best to default to the two Gertrudes here: An artist of gardens themselves, Gertrude Jekyll's sage observation that a gardener is to "acquire a knowledge of what to do, but also to gain some wisdom in perceiving what it is well to let alone" is a more active version of Gertrude Stein's penultimate definition: "Rose is a

rose is a rose." Since Shakespeare populates his prose and poetry with Roses far more than with any other flower, he can speak for himself on their infinite variety. In and among his many mentions, there are a few specific flowers that warrant some brief delineation:

⚘ RED ROSE ‒ [*Rosa gallica*] also crimson, vermillion; *see also* YORK/LANCASTER ROSES.

⚘ DAMASK ROSE ‒ [*Rosa damascena*] with origins in Damascus; scent inspired the proverb "sweet as Damask Roses"; often compared to complexion; Gerard says it is "of a pale red colour and of a more pleasant smell, and fitter for meate or medicine."

⚘ WHITE ROSE ‒ [*Rosa alba*] technically, never satisfactorily identified; Lys de Bray, in her charming book *Fantastic Garlands*, calls it "a perfumed tangle of rose history that will never be fully unravelled."

⚘ PROVINCIAL/ PROVENÇAL ROSE ‒ [*Rosa centifolia*] reference Provence, France. When Hamlet refers to it, he means to be provocative, flashy, affected. Gerard calls it the great Holland Rose; a.k.a. Cabbage Rose.

⚘ MUSK-ROSE ‒ [*Rosa arvensis*] a.k.a. Trailing Rose; prized more for its unique scent than for its beauty.

⚘ ROSE OF MAY ‒ [*Rosa majalis*] Gerard calls this the Cinnamon or Cannell Rose.

⚘ ROSE ‒ [*Rosa canina*] a wild climbing rose; older folk names include Dogberry and Witch's Brier; *see also* THORNS.

⚘ BRIAR ROSE ‒ a.k.a. Scotch Rose; *see* BRIERS, EGLANTINE, also THORNS on roses.

⚘ CAKES of ROSES, ROSE WATER ‒ as Roses were considered the penultimate beauty, they were used then, as now, for cosmetic purposes; looking to the Doctrine of Signatures, like to like, to use the Rose was to become the Rose.

❧ *WAR OF THE ROSES* ❧

⚘ RED AND WHITE ROSES were the emblems of the HOUSES OF LANCASTER and YORK. With the roses alone: A long scene in Act II of *Henry VI, Part 1*, establishes the conflict, lighted on in Act IV, with more rose conflict in *Henry VI, Part 3*, then the resolve in the last act of *Richard III*, in a speech by Richmond, the future King Henry VII, which will unite the factions of Plantagenet, and form the Tudor Rose ... and the Tudor Dynasty. What's remarkable? The tension is clear through only the mention of Roses. And the idea that they are fighting with flowers.

ROSEMARY ‑ Dew of the sea [*Rosmarinus*] invokes the bracing fragrance of this multiuse herb. Prized for its culinary, medicinal, and cosmetic applications. Shakespeare cites it most often as an herb of remembrance. Used for strengthening the memory, the scent became a kindle to lost energy; a BACHELOR'S BUTTON of sorts to make a lovers' tryst more memorable; a reminder of the dearly departed; even rubbed on the head to remind hair to grow.

RUE / HERB of GRACE ‑ The grace that follows repentance or regret is what connects the two names for this garden plant. Cultivated for medicinal uses, the yellow flowers and bluish green leaves emit a powerfully pungent scent that Shakespeare alternately describes as "sour" or sweet "nose-herbs." Gerard cites it as an antidote for Wolfsbane [ACONITUM] and toxic MUSHROOMS.

RUSHES / BULRUSH ‑ An array of marsh plants with stiff, often hollow stems, which, when filled with animal fat, made poor men's candles. Practical domestic use included carpeting the floors of the wealthy to absorb smells and mask dirt. Rush rings, made from the stems, served as marriage tokens for common folk [often sans the ceremony]; Lavatch twists the rush ring custom into a bawdy joke. The Bulrush, a.k.a. Sweet Sedge [*illustrated below*], cited in *Two Noble Kinsmen*, could almost suggest dredlocks. *See also* REEDS, SEDGE, and GRASSES.

RYE ‑ A crop akin to WHEAT but considered inferior, even though it's sturdier and more tolerant of less-than-optimum conditions.

S

SAFFRON ‑ It takes the yellow stigmas of nine crocuses to get one grain of good saffron, that's over four thousand flowers for one ounce. This accounts for its high cost, but it was still a less-expensive option than the gold leaf used for manuscript illumination. In turn, MARIGOLDS were an even cheaper knockoff of the coveted deep golden food coloring. Saffron Walden, in Essex, was named for the plentiful crop, as was Saffron Hill in the Camden area of London.

SAMPHIRE ‑ a.k.a. Sea Fennel, it grows on cliff sides. Its name is thought to be an Anglicized "herbe St. Pierre"—St. Peter's symbol being a rock jutting out from the sea. In *King Lear*, Edgar plays What Job Would I Hate? as he feigns watching a harvester of the succulent plant. Gerard was a fan: "The leaves kept in pickle and eaten in sallads with oile and vinegar . . .

wholesome for the stoppings of the liver, milt and kidnies. It is the pleasantest sauce . . . best agreeing with man's body."

SAVORY ‑ Highly aromatic, this hardy Mediterranean herb is included in Perdita's list of "middle summer" flowers "given to men of middle age," perhaps partly because its juice was thought to cure "dimness of the eyes," according to botanist Nicholas Culpeper. "Mercury claims dominion over this herb," he notes, believing that Summer Savory was better than Winter.

SEDGE ‑ Growing on watery banks and in marshy areas, it can be both an individual plant and a plurality of coarse GRASSES and RUSH-like plants; it is assumed that Shakespeare employs a more generic use.

SENNA ‑ see CYME.

SPEAR-GRASS ‑ Several options have been posited as the plant that Bardolph [*Henry IV*] suggests for use to induce a nosebleed. Pictured is Couch-grass [crossed with Horsetail], for its long, slender reed lined with rough spikelets. *See* GRASSES.

SQUASH ‑ see PEAS.

STRAWBERRY ‑ A native, low-growing fruit, the small alpine version is found in the wild and in cultivated gardens, such as at the estate of the Bishops of Ely in Holborn. The Strawberries grown there were said to be the best in London; Shakespeare includes this local lore in both *Henry V* and *Richard III*. The berry was also a popular motif for embroidery, although with contradictory symbolism: purity and innocence vs. sexuality and jealousy—all of that is in play when it appears, fatally so, on Desdemona's handkerchief.

STUBBLE – see **WHEAT**.

SUGAR – This inclusion was tenuous, given that sugar is a refined product removed from the original Sugarcane plant. But . . . it *is* a plant. Gerard had a go at growing it and Reverend Ellacombe believes Shakespeare may have seen it. So, included are the quotes that seem to refer to the actual substance, not the adjective [i.e., "sugar'd words," although the line of demarcation can be fuzzy]. As noted in **ALMOND**, Elizabethans' passion for sugar led them to candy nuts [sweetmeats], flowers, and seeds [comfits]; make sirrops,

suckets [candied fruit peels], and jellies. Banquets featured sugarplate, crafted from sugar paste and egg white, elaborately decorated and personalized, sometimes with a poem. Known for her sweet tooth, Queen Elizabeth was gifted with a sugar-plate castle and sugar loaves [cone-shaped solid sugar for transport, which was then shaved or chunked], plus a barrel of sucket in the 1560s. By 1598, a German visitor reported "her Teeth black, a defect the English seem subject to, from their too great use of sugar."

SYCAMORE – Although scholars have debated precisely

which tree is meant in Shakespeare's three references, a homophonic approach might be more rewarding: *syc-amore* = sick of love. Certainly Desdemona's melancholy melody notes her grief over Othello's mind diseased with jealousy; *Love's Labour's Lost*'s aloof, self-loving French courtier Boyet only reports on others' amatory imbroglios; Benvolio seeks out Romeo to assuage his heartsickness over Rosaline. Curiously, the "grove of sycamore" where he spots his friend "westward" of "this city side" actually existed in Verona; some trees still stand by the western wall today.

T

THISTLE – Invasive weed covered with pricks and a globular head inviting to bees, the Thistle is handsome enough to be the floral emblem of Scotland. *Thistle* can be a generic term for an array of prickly plants; in *Henry V* they are an indication of neglect. Donkeys are the only animals that feed on Thistles, so there's an embedded joke in Bottom's directive. *See also* **CARDUUS BENEDICTUS/ HOLY THISTLE**.

THORNS – Any sharp-pointed spires or prickles on the stems, leaves, or heads of plants, or the plants themselves. These dangers

lie in underbrush, thicket, deep woods, or a deceptive garden. Or metaphorically, such as in Gertrude's heart. Ours include **BLACKBERRY** bramble, Milk **THISTLE**, **HAWTHORN**, and Scotch **ROSE**. *See also* **BRIERS**.

THYME – The three references in Shakespeare to this fragrant herb neatly encompass the three kinds of thyme: Oberon's native variety, found on sandy heaths; Iago's garden version of Mediterranean origin in his screed on health and personal responsibility; and finally, the Song in *Two Noble*

Kinsmen that gives echo to Time itself as well as the strewing herb.

TOADSTOOL – see **MUSHROOM**.

TURNIP – This "potherb" gets one mention in Shakespeare, and usually a big laugh, when Anne Page prefers Death by Vegetable to marrying a foolish suitor in *Merry Wives of Windsor*. Cultivated for centuries, mostly as animal fodder, the [vitamin-rich] leaves were more frequently served at table, while roots were carved into "characters," as Imogen does in *Cymbeline*.

V

VETCHES [see **WHEAT**] – Pretty enough to warrant its own page, Vetch's delicate beauty also has a function: improving the soil of **WHEAT** fields. A legume in

the **PEA** family, Vetches are also cultivated for forage, presumably why Iris [goddess of the rainbow and a plant herself! *See* **FLAGS**] includes it in her invocation of

abundance for the young lovers of *The Tempest*.

VINE – When Shakespeare speaks of vines, he always means the grapevine—a symbol of fruitfulness [see GRAPES] or lack thereof, as when Adriana calls herself a Vine in need of her husband as an ELM to twine around. Vines and vineyards [which we omitted here] also symbolized possession and productivity.

VIOLET – Its fresh perfume alone inspires five mentions, but the tiny, delicately veined wildflower is also imbued with qualities of humility, gentleness, and faithfulness [a clue to Viola's character in *Twelfth Night*, and conversely so for Malvolio]. PANSIES and other flowers of similar color were sometimes called Violets. Perhaps because of its drooping head, the Violet was considered virtuous, soporific, and an antidote to anger. An edible flower, the leaves and petals often graced salads and were paired with Onion dishes.

W

WALNUT – Not much is made of the mighty Walnut tree in Shakespeare, although it is suggested that his many mentions of NUTS generically could include the Walnut kernel. No, he refers to the capacious shell [comparatively speaking] as a hiding place or plaything. But the meat of the nut was enjoyed as a savory snack, or sugared for a sweetmeat.

WARDEN – see PEAR.

WHEAT / STUBBLE [see also VETCHES] – Wheat is the queen of crops—bread made from pure Wheat was a rare luxury; though near in kin to RYE and BARLEY, they were considered poor relations; CORN was an umbrella term for all three, and grain in general. STUBBLE refers to the threshed fields, primarily Wheat, but other grains as well. Wheat symbolized fertility and the bounty of the earth; to wear a wheaten garland indicated peace and plenty. The greening of Wheat was a sign of spring, a portent of abundance to come.

WILLOW / OSIER – The traditional weeping willow we often picture doesn't actually arrive on the scene until c. 1700, but that hasn't stopped artists from painting poor Ophelia beside one. Her "pendant boughs" may have been the "crack willow" due to its branches' tendency to break suddenly. The Common Osier [*Salix viminalis*], with its slightly narrower leaves, was used interchangeably with WILLOW for basket weaving and garland making—wearing a Willow garland [or just singing about it, as Desdemona does] suggests grieving for lost love. In England, Willow was sometimes a stand-in on Palm Sunday for the Palm branches in church processions.

WOODBINE – see HONEYSUCKLE.

WORMWOOD / DIAN'S BUD – Considered the mother of all herbs [in the mugwort family], and associated with Artemis, goddess of pregnancy [or her Roman counterpart, Diana], its bitter taste helped wean breast-feeding children, as the Nurse natters on about in her bawdy reminiscence of Juliet. One of the nine sacred herbs of the *Lacnunga*, an Anglo-Saxon herbal, it was an antidote to toxic TOADSTOOLS, and a barrier to moths and fleas on clothing and bed linen. Oberon applies it as a cure for lovesickness; it is a primary ingredient in vermouth and absinthe.

Y

YEW – This native tree is a traditional symbol of mourning. It appears six times in Shakespeare [maybe seven, surreptitiously], always to do with death; its appearance onstage could be a harbinger of poisoning, such as Balthasar and Paris citing Yew trees in the churchyard, while in the nearby tomb Romeo drank poison. Its evergreen foliage is fatal, as are the seeds [though not their red casing]. Yew is the strongest candidate for the HEBENON / HEBONA poison in *Hamlet*.

** Our petals now are ended . . .**

ACKNOWLEDGMENTS

First of all, I am grateful for the elegant and evocative images by artist Sumié Hasegawa, which made me realize that *actually* seeing *all* the plants was not only enormously helpful, it didn't exist anywhere. I'm thankful for her curiosity, which grew into obsession [I get that!]; her helpful husband, Fred Collins, who started her down the garden path; and their trust in me to create a trellis, if you will, for these plants to thrive; and to our mutual friend David Tabatsky, whose brainstorm brought us together. I'm always grateful for Stacy Prince, here in particular for her editorial insight and for connecting me with my smart and patient agent, Coleen O'Shea, and thence my enthusiastic and understanding editor extraordinaire, Becca Hunt.

I'm in awe of those who tirelessly burrow down tunnels of research, often without appreciation, for folks like me to pick up kernels here and there, so I'd like to throw some shine on Jane Lawson, whose decades of work on Queen Elizabeth's Gift Rolls added delightful color and texture here; Ros Barber for generously sharing her prepublication insights on Honey-stalks and Warwickshire dialect; Eddi Jolly's deep dive into *Hamlet;* logophilic author Howard Richler; Michael Marcus, who located the perfect quote; Julia Cleave's rose insights; Dorna Bewley's willingness to wade into the weeds with me; Dr. Bríd McGrath for just about anything; and the many garden conversations I had with the late Dr. John Rollett.

Research institutions are made up of remarkable individuals; I am honored to have occasion to be in their debt: Librarian Simon Blundell at the Reform Club; Dr. Mark Spencer at London's Natural History Museum; the accommodating staff at the Linnean Society of London; Ortrun Peyn at London's Society of Antiquaries; Jennifer Lee at Columbia University's Butler Library; Wallace et al. in Rare Books at the British Library; and all the wonderful folk at the Folger Shakespeare Library, especially Owen Williams, Betsy Walsh, Camille Seerattan, Alan Katz, and garden docent Marya Fitzgerald—who probably aren't even aware of what their contributions seed.

My fantastic team: Bronwyn Berry, Megan Cooper, Morgan Millogo, for helping me keep track of a million minute details, plus making a floor-to-ceiling floral mosaic of the office. For their generosity of time, materials, and expertise, my many thanks to Andrew French, David Cole Wheeler, Neil Martin; weedy exchanges with Jan Cole, and especially Rebecca Webb Serou, who apparently stays up as late as I do.

Finally, with a hat-tip to Proust, to the "charming gardeners who make our souls blossom," mine anyway [which includes many of the above] Marty Ittner and Keith Berner, Lisa Alberti, Brandon Judell, Patsy & Co., Peter Judd, Theodore Melendez, Kate Konigisor and Katrina Ferguson, Nancy and Simon Jones, and Gail Colson, Shari Hoffman, Sherry Anderson, John Augustine and Christopher Durang.

And, unexpectedly, to the 2015 Spenser Conference in Ireland, where, tramping through pastures to find Edmund Spenser's rubble heap of a castle, I suddenly noticed the fields were full of the very plants on these pages! Including stinging nettles. The delightful pain of research offered the experience of time travel.

—Gerit Quealy

My initial dream was to paint the entire collection of Shakespeare's botanicals. I would like to acknowledge the Bond Street Theatre Coalition's theatrical productions as my initial inspiration. I am very grateful to my college friend Uchida Shinji for his enthusiasm and technical help. A big hug to Simon O'Leary for providing shelter on my many trips to London. With the help of my husband, Fred, who thought of the title for this book, and our friend and colleague David Tabatsky, who moved this forward and led us to Gerit Quealy, Coleen O'Shea, and HarperCollins, I have finally been able to see it happen. I am very grateful to each of them for helping me get here. I hope you will enjoy viewing the art in this book as much as I enjoyed creating it.

Domo arigato gozaimashita,
—Sumié Hasegawa-Collins

GO TO:

www.BotanicalShakespeare.com

FOR THE PLANTS LISTED
by Play, by Character, and by Species

- PLUS -
Bibliography, Footnotes, Fun Facts & more!